Hollingsworth

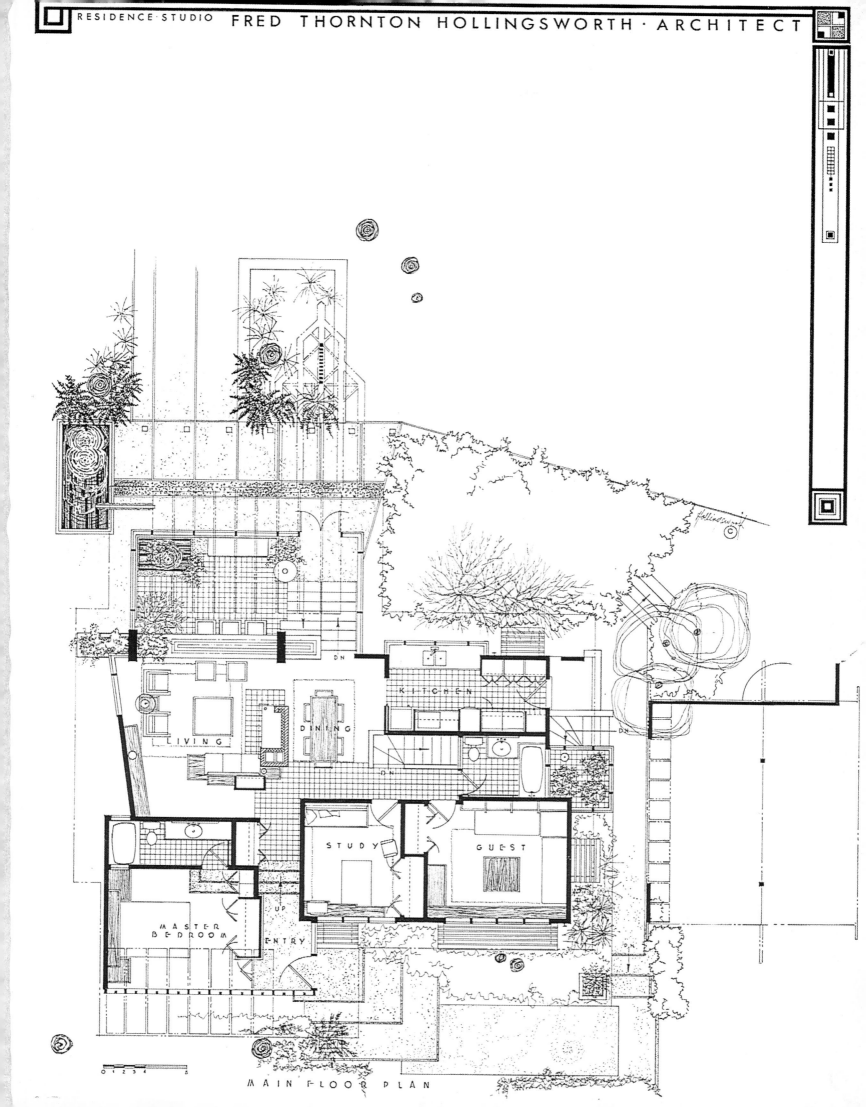

RESIDENCE·STUDIO FRED THORNTON HOLLINGSWORTH · ARCHITECT

KITCHEN

DINING

LIVING

STUDY

GUEST

MASTER BEDROOM

ENTRY

UP

DN

0 1 2 3 4 5

MAIN FLOOR PLAN

Hollingsworth 1946
1960
1979

# Living Spaces

# THE ARCHITECTURE OF FRED THORNTON

# HOLLINGSWORTH

BLUE*im*PRINT

# contents

# Preface

WHEN FRED HOLLINGSWORTH AND I FIRST ENTERED INTO PARTNERSHIP IN 1963, HE WAS ALREADY COMMITTED to architecture of organic modernism. I found his bold residential designs stimulating and admired his passionate reverence for nature and the land.

Fred found his inspiration (as I did four years later) in the office of Thompson Berwick and Pratt, the leading post-war design firm in the city. TBP's work load was enormous in those halcyon days and talented new employees, including Fred, Ron Thom, Arthur Erickson, Geoff Massey and Bob Burniston were handed full design responsibilities for house commissions that Ned Pratt and Bob Berwick could not handle themselves. Utilizing drafting experience gained in the aeronautic and sheet mental industry, Fred's creative skills flourished. As well, he, like all the budding architects of the day, had a thorough understanding of the tenets of celebrated architects Bernard Maybeck, Harwell Harris, Frank Lloyd Wright and Richard Neutra.

It was at the Neutra design sessions held in the 1950's at artist-teacher Bert Binnings home, that I first met Fred – then later at Cris and Ron Thom's new home in upper Lynn Valley. At these events, Ron and Fred's artist friends, Fred Amess, Jack Shadbolt, Don Jarvis, Rudy Kovacks and others, often held the floor. Topics varied, new technology, landscape, painting, colour, furnishings and ceramics, were as likely subjects for discussion as planning or architecture. Design for living was paramount. Neutra, on the other hand, majestically espoused his "survival through design" theories which suited our west coast sensibilities: Human physiology as it related to the quality of our built environment. It was heady and riveting stuff.

For Hollingsworth, Thom, and Ned Pratt their mentor, all aspects of planning, architecture, art and livability were considered… climatic impact; the mysteries and delights of the site; flexible building programs, use of new technology and materials, and the incorporation of art and artisans. Total design control was essential, including interior design, integral furnishings – even landscaping. The ranch house vernacular soon gave way to the contemporary modular and nuclear home. The accepted unit of measurement became the 4 x 8 plywood sheet. Concrete block, heated concrete floors, timber posts, beams and decking and flat tar and gravel roofs were incorporated. All were cost effective as the modern house became more affordable.

Many of Fred Hollingsworth's structures in the Capilano Highlands featured a central fireplace, the heart of his small one level houses. In some version, fireplaces were set in cave-like recesses, implying protective "hearths", warmth and personal comfort. At this time new geometries were explored, square, circular and later, triangular forms. Shifted volumes and raised "floating" roofs caused a new interior spatial dynamic. High clerestory windows provided overhead light penetration and French doors and floor to ceiling glass openings were oriented to the rear of the property for family privacy and views of garden or forest. These design innovations were considered radical in their day and became part of Fred's creative dogma for over fifty years of practice. When I arrived at the Hollingsworth studio there was instant rapport. We had similar interests, drawing, watercolours, photography and an affinity for landscape design and Japanese building typologies. Together we enjoyed a healthy exchange of ideas. Individually we undertook two house designs in West Vancouver, vowing to save most of the tress on site. One house crowned the brow of a hill and the other bridged a steep slope swale. Both were narrow, long profiles curved towards the view, and we adopted a vocabulary of thin roof members and white stucco walls to capture sunlight and tree shadows. Like the Japanese house, we tied the interiors together at door height with a continuous board of cedar, separating the strip of wall above – the kokabe – as part of the raised ceiling form. Handmade lanterns were made for each building. We were fortunate to win two Massey Medals in 1964, for our efforts.

During these years clients were found to build four innovative medical clinics where small outdoor walled garden "rooms" animated or provided a calming atmosphere to adjacent waiting areas and examining rooms. It was all part of a growing concern for more humane spaces and a socially responsive architecture. Sometimes lattice screens were devised, in Kyoto fashion, to modulate space and natural light, or used for textural reason. Wood screens, in various design formats, became a Hollingsworth trademark on important hotel and residential projects.

When I left the partnership, Fred launched into the most prolific and creative period in his life. With larger commissions, he was able to explore more inventive compositions – and build in concrete. Here he displayed a keen sense of the material, its plasticity, structural capabilities, and the textural and sculptural opportunities it afforded. Witness the magnificent concrete trellis, and lush hammered and shuttered wall of the University of B.C. Faculty of Law Building. An oneness of material pervades in a heavy-use student setting. All wrapped around a striking inner garden court.

Further imaginative monolithic constructions emerge in Fred's residences of the 1970's to 90's. Heroic forms, some a cubist assembly of projected volumes, wall planes and gardens; others curvilinear, echoing the lay of the land or standing proud of it. Many of the houses are eco-sensitive, shaped in new-found geometries to deal with prairie winds, planted roofs and topographical intrusions.

I was able to walk through the Bosa Residence with Fred a few years ago, just before its completion. I think of this unique structure as one of his later-day masterworks but he would have none of it. Even so, the project reveals all that is distinctive about Fred's work, in this instance an original expression of dynamic form at the edge of the sea. "Two seashells" establish the motif and complement the rounded shapes of weathered rock on site. Circular drums of concrete and glass anchor the house to the land. Within, a two-level fireplace centers the composition and etched glass walls display abstract wave-like, sea scalloped patterns. Full of light and energy, there is a magic quality here, reflecting the persona of both the owners and architect.

Fred Thornton Hollingsworth, architect, artist and artisan, is still designing and painting, often consulting with Russell Hollingsworth, his gifted architect son. Conceptualizing, drawing, and constructing delicate model airplanes from his residence/studio (which is itself a rich compendium of his art work, furniture, and spatial delights) he is assisted, as always, by Phyllis, his charming wife, advisor and unfailing supporter. Holding true to organic principles, Fred continues to build houses that serve busy family lives – robust, stable, warm and spirited environments which indeed enhance the life of their inhabitants. His remarkable legacy lies within the pages of this book and, as with all exemplary work, points towards new possibilities in architecture and liveability. ▦

Barry Downs
*January 3, 2005*

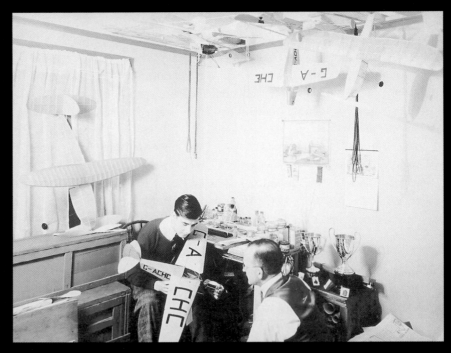

by Greg Bellerby

FRED HOLLINGSWORTH WAS BORN IN ENGLAND IN 1917, AND THE FAMILY IMMIGRATED TO CANADA IN 1929. They settled in Vancouver where Hollingsworth's mother's sisters and brother had already established themselves. His father was a herbalist and had a store in Oldham near Manchester before coming to Canada. In Vancouver, his father was employed on the stationmaster's staff for the CPR. Hollingsworth grew up in the Marpole area and attended Point Grey Junior High School and Magee High School. As a young person he was interested in two things: model airplanes and music. Among his high school acquaintances was Dal Richards, who later became one of the best-known band leaders on the West Coast; they played and sang in the high school band together. Ron Thom, who became a renowned architect and life-long friend, also attended Magee. Thom was also interested in music and aspired to be a classical pianist. Although they were not good friends at the time, their paths would cross again in the future.

Hollingsworth's interest in building model airplanes and competing has been a life-long pursuit. In 1935 and 1936 he was a Canadian National champion, travelling as far as Toronto to compete. He continued to be involved with airplanes, building models, competing in national and international flying competitions, learning to fly, and owning his own aircraft, a Cessna 182.

When Hollingsworth got out of high school work was scarce, but he was able to get a job as an apprentice sheet metal worker with Western Steel Products, where his Uncle George was the foreman of the production area. He served his apprenticeship and became a skilled sheet metal worker. Hollingsworth remembers the experience as wonderful because, "It instilled in me the value of working, really working." [1]

1. Fred Hollingsworth, interview excerpt, 2004.

At the start of World War II, Boeing Aircraft set up a factory in Vancouver for the production of the PBY airplane, which was a twin-engine flying boat. Fred's Uncle George had left Western Steel to become shop superintendent at the Boeing plant. Hollingsworth soon followed, and his skill as a sheet metal worker and his model airplane experience made for a good fit with Boeing. He was later given the opportunity to set up the production illustration department. The department's activity was to convert technical drawings into perspectives which would be easier to read by inexperienced workers. A large part of the work was creating repair manuals for the Canadian PBY. The plane's design changed rapidly, so the manuals had to be constantly updated. Hollingsworth was in charge of up to 150 workers, and half of them were doing design changes. Working at Boeing sparked Fred's interest in graphics, books, and printing, which appealed to him because he always had the ability to draw. "I met interesting people, architects and engineers, and it changed my perspective on what I wanted to do with my life." [2]

2. Ibid.

After the war, Hollingsworth headed up the art department for Mann Litho Company. He had also formed a jazz band called the Fred Hollingworth Orchestra in which he played tenor saxophone and sang. The band performed at many of the dance clubs in Vancouver. He was friends with several of the best musicians in the city; Dal Richards from his high school days, Lance Harrison, and Mart Kenney were all part of the circle at that time. Hollingsworth acknowledges that the music business life-style was demanding and very difficult to maintain. Around this time he met and married Phyllis Montgomery, who not only became his life-long partner, but also an important part of his future architectural practice. They wanted to move out of their small apartment in the city, so they purchased a lot in the Capilano Highlands development in North Vancouver. He decided to try his hand at designing their house.

Hollingsworth had been introduced to the work of Frank Lloyd Wright while at Boeing, and he had also looked at houses designed by Paul Thiery in Seattle who had been developing a simple open plan approach. Once the plans were completed, they had to be approved by the firm of Thompson, Berwick and Pratt, who were over-seeing the designs for Capilano Highlands. "I went to their office and met with Ned Pratt, who commented that the drawings

Opposite page top to bottom:
Fred and his father,
Boeing aircraft, production
illustration department and
the Fred Hollingsworth Orchestra

were pretty good. He asked who the architect was and after hearing I had done them myself, Pratt asked if I had ever thought about being an architect. Saying yes, Pratt then suggested that I come to work for them and see about becoming an architect." [3]

*3. Fred Hollingsworth, interview excerpt, 2004.*

Fred started working for C.J. Thompson as a draftsman and began learning the practical aspects of architecture. Along with commercial buildings such as banks, the firm specialized in schools, and Ned Pratt and Bob Berwick had designed an efficient and inexpensive post and beam school structure. They built schools all over British Columbia. Not long after Hollingsworth had started with the firm, Ron Thom came into the office as an apprentice, also with the intent of becoming an architect. They became life-long friends and the firm's best designers. Thom became one of the most esteemed architects in Canada, leaving a legacy of buildings and houses on the West Coast and in Ontario, where he later set up his own practice.

The firm of Thompson, Berwick and Pratt was one of the most successful architectural firms in Vancouver. They got most of the interesting commissions at that time and were therefore able to attract the brightest young architects and designers. In his biography of Ron Thom, Douglas Shadbolt writes about the firm, saying, "Although the atmosphere was highly competitive, the senior partners relied on and favoured the self-starter who understood the implicit message coded in the firm's policy. These individuals had no doubt that this firm was winning the most interesting commissions in the city and was open to experimentation with the modernist ideas of the day". [4] In an article titled "Thompson, Berwick and Pratt", published in Canadian Architect in 1961, Ned Pratt frames the firm's policy with statements such as, "The acceptance of the principle of change," and, "Great freedom exists within the firm for both staff and partners." [5] Thompson, Berwick and Pratt were a virtual greenhouse of talented architects during the 1950's.

*4. Douglas Shadbolt, Ron Thom: The Shaping of an Architect, (Vancouver/Toronto: Douglas & McIntyre, 1995), p.17.*
*5. Ned Pratt, "Thompson, Berwick and Pratt," Canadian Architect (June 1961), vol.6, p.55.*

Sky Bungalow

Both Hollingsworth and Thom were fully engaged in this hotbed of new ideas and approaches circulating through the firm, particularly by Ned Pratt, who was a champion of modernism. Hollingsworth and Thom made several trips both together and apart to study first-hand the houses and buildings they had read about, and to meet the influential architects of the time. Hollingsworth drove across the country to meet Frank Lloyd Wright at Taliesin east and west. Wright's design and architectural principles were to have a lasting influence on Hollingsworth's work and shaped his philosophy of architecture. Hollingsworth participated in many of the firm's famous Friday afternoon discussions between the partners, staff, and visitors. With the high volume of commissions and an open and encouraging policy, surrounded by intelligent and engaged colleagues, Thompson, Berwick and Pratt was an exceptional place for someone to learn and practice the skills of architecture.

Working as a draftsman did not pay well in those days and there was no overtime pay, so Hollingsworth arranged it with Bob Berwick in order that he could design houses at home in the evenings. Eric Allan, the developer of Capilano Highlands, began sending clients to Hollingsworth; and this relationship was to continue for many years. One of these projects was to become quite significant. Allan had the idea to build a promotional house downtown in partnership with the Hudson's Bay store. The house would be constructed on the parking lot and people would be charged ten cents to tour it, with the money going to the symphony. The manager of the store agreed, but stipulated that the house could only take up three parking spaces. Hollingsworth came up with the idea of supporting the house on beams and floating it over the cars. The *Sky Bungalow*, as it was called, was a huge success and introduced aspects of modern design that would become features of West Coast residential architecture. The house incorporated many of the organic principals with which Hollingsworth had been working. This meant, among other things, that "the space below [the ground], is just as important as space above. The whole building belongs to the site, in an organic sense. It should look as if it grew there and is just as comfortable as the plants are." 6

6. Fred Hollingsworth, interview excerpt, 2004.

Eric Allan was somewhat unique as a developer at that time. He brought an approach to Capilano Highlands that left the landscape as untouched as possible. He made building lots of different sizes to suit the terrain, rather than clearing the site, left the trees, and did not culvert and fill in the creeks. This sensitivity to the natural environment is a rare occurrence even today. Over the years Allan sent many clients to Hollingsworth, which gave him an opportunity to design houses that were economical as well as innovative. His *Neoteric* houses were post-and-beam construction with an open plan that utilized a concrete slab floor with radiant warm-air heating, The houses were often oriented away from the street toward the garden at the rear of the lot. Hollingsworth applied the principles of organic architecture in the construction of the houses and their relation to the building site. In all he designed about fifty houses in Capilano Highlands.

Upon leaving TB&P in 1952, Hollingsworth went to work for William Birmingham as an associate. While working with Birmingham, he designed many projects, including a Native Museum in Prince Rupert, a hotel and general store in Hazelton, and the Red Feather Building in Vancouver. At that time the office was located in a former drug store on Davie Street. Bud Wood, a young architect who had just graduated from the University of Oregon, came to work in the office. He and Hollingsworth became friends and travelled several times to Portland, Oregon where he met architects such as John Yeon and Peitro Beluschi, both influential in the development of modern architecture in that region. He also made trips to San Francisco where he met Bernard Maybeck, then in his eighties, whom Hollingsworth held in great esteem for his classical/modernism. Bud Wood also encouraged Hollingsworth to study and write his architect's exams.

Top: Neoteric House

Bottom: Red Feather Building

Although Fred was recognized as a great designer, he still sought to be an architect. He wrote his exams and was finally registered in 1959. Shortly thereafter he left Birmingham and set up his own practice in his North Vancouver home.

His first major commission was the Imperial Hotel in Victoria. The clients had requested that the design have a Japanese feel. Both Hollingsworth and Ron Thom had an interest in and studied Oriental architecture because of its many ties to organic architecture. Along with its oriental touches, forms that made connections to nature were incorporated. The hotel received critical acclaim for its design and was also a financial success for its owners.

The practice was growing, and Hollingsworth was able to attract many open-minded clients. Some of the more significant houses that were constructed at that time were the Trethewey house in 1959, which was the first time that Hollingsworth used circular forms in a design. The McGrath house in Seattle in 1960 provided an opportunity to realize a completely integrated design, which included a number of ornamental details and even its own unique furniture. He later designed a guest pavilion next to the original house in 1969. In these two houses one can see an attention to detail and finish that had not previously been present. This can be attributed to clients' desires and ability to afford high quality materials and finish in the design and construction of their houses.

The Berkeley Hospital of 1960 was also a major project for Hollingsworth and an opportunity to create an innovative design approach to facilities for the care of the elderly, one that had a supportive environment. This hospital became a model; Hollingsworth designed a number of them based on the ideas that the elderly should be treated with dignity and respect, and that their living environment should allow for comfort and stimulation. Along with basic nursing requirements, the facilities had workshops and gardens for the use of the residents.

In 1962 Hollingsworth formed a partnership with Barry Downs. At the time Downs was working at TB&P and had graduated from the University of Washington. Hollingsworth knew Downs socially and had admired his work. As well they shared a similar philosophy, and Downs had worked with Ron Thom at TB&P. Fred approached Downs with the idea of a partnership and he agreed. Hollingsworth had expanded the office at home, but soon they were busy and needed more space. He had designed a small medical building in West Vancouver and they moved into offices there on Clyde Avenue. Together they worked on a number of hospitals and residences, and at one point employed four draftsmen, including Walter Wiltshire and Rob Way who continued to work for Downs after he set up his own practice. In 1962 they were awarded the Massey Medal for the Maltby Residence. Constructed into a rocky site in West Vancouver, the house had a Japanese sensibility while retaining a connection to the West Coast contemporary aesthetic. The Frackson house, also designed at this time, incorporated an open floor plan and a wonderful integration of indoor and outdoor spaces.

Hollingsworth had never wanted to develop a large firm and was really only interested in the work that he thought he could control. He saw the pressures of managing a large staff as an enormous responsibility. Downs, on the other hand, wanted the firm to expand and was interested in seeking major projects within the city. In 1966 they dissolved the partnership, allowing Downs to pursue larger projects and Hollingsworth to pursue the work that most satisfied him. They have remained close friends over the years.

For some time Hollingsworth maintained his office on Clyde Avenue, later moving back home after creating a new office/studio. He states that the advantage of working from home is that, "You can work day and night," [7] which he did. Another advantage to staying small was the control over the design process. Fred always did his own working drawings and believed in the value of drawing. "I think you develop your own style through working drawings. You develop a sensitivity to the minor things that change a space or material." [8]

Top to bottom:
Trethewey house,
McGrath house and
Berkeley Hospital

Maltby residence

In 1971 Hollingsworth completed work on the University of B.C., Faculty of Law Building. The all-concrete structure was designed around a large open courtyard. One of the important aspects of the design for Hollingsworth was to create an opportunity for a greater interrelationship between faculty and students. He achieved this by separating the classrooms and library from the faculty offices, but linking them with a circulation corridor. Students were able to intercept the faculty as they moved through the corridor.

Over the next twenty-five years Hollingsworth, for the most part, concentrated on residential architecture and developed a great many loyal and supportive clients. The result is an inventory of thoughtfully designed and beautifully constructed residences. Each house reflects the principles of organic design that first inspired Hollingsworth to become involved with architecture.

*7. Fred Hollingsworth, interview excerpt, 2004.*

*8. Ibid.*

UBC Faculty of Law Building

He found great satisfaction in residential design. "It is the only work where you have to have an intimate relationship with the client. You have to know all about them to be able to design a really nice house for them." [9] He goes on to say, "Space affects people, makes them feel comfortable or not. I think it is important that people relate to the spaces they are in. If they are good spaces it teaches you so much about nature itself. Living in a well-designed environment teaches you to look for things, to become aware of space and details." [10] This awareness of the importance of space and its effects have guided Hollingsworth's designs from the first house he did for himself and his wife Phyllis through to his last houses, the Bosa House of 1990 and the Kassam House of 1994. His intent was to create a space that is "a true expression of the materials used to form it and [which] offers comfort and delight to its users." [11]

An important aspect of Hollingsworth's practice was the involvement of his wife Phyllis. They shared their domestic life, but Phyllis was also involved with the business, taking responsibility for the records and the finances. Hollingsworth readily acknowledges the support and contribution that Phyllis made to the success of the architectural practice.

Fred Hollingsworth also contributed to the professional side of architecture through his involvement with the Architectural Institute of B.C. and later the Royal Architectural Institute of Canada. He first became a council member of the A.I.B.C. in 1965, and was asked to serve on a committee organizing a national conference being held in Vancouver. Hollingsworth was always interested and engaged with the larger issues and concerns of architecture, and the conference provided an opportunity to meet most of the important architects of the time. He was elected President of the A.I.B.C. in 1971 and served a two-year term. A fellow and council member of

9. *Fred Hollingsworth, interview excerpt, 2004.*

10. *Ibid.*

11. *Ibid.*

the Royal Architectural Institute of Canada from 1971 to 1974, in 1975 he was elected President for a two-year term. When speaking of his involvement with the Institutes, he mentions his desire to repay the architectural profession for the opportunities it had given him. "I thought the organization could do great things for the public by informing them about architecture and what it really was all about. It has a role to play in lobbying the government; researching and developing financing for young people. I saw that it had potential and could be a positive influence on many levels." [12]

12. Fred Hollingsworth, interview excerpt, 2004.

In 1953, Hollingsworth ran as a candidate for the North Vancouver District Council and was elected Alderman, citing the need to address the issue of increased industrial growth. He was instrumental in establishing the first Planning Department, which would oversee the development of the District. His work for the Architectural Institute and the District of North Vancouver reflects his sense of responsibility toward both the community he works with, and the community he lives in.

In the last few years Hollingsworth has turned his attention to the problems of sustainability and the environment in regards to domestic architecture. He has developed what he calls the *Environmatic House*. The design is an attempt to create an environmentally friendly building using the technology of today. The living spaces are oriented around a large central atrium, which serves as an indoor landscape as well as a solar heat collector. The house uses no fossil fuels for heating, and attempts by the use of other innovative processes, such as recycling sewage water, to affect the environment as little as possible. "It is intended to create a new experience in spatial living and a more natural environment for its occupants." [13]

13. Ibid.

Hollingsworth designed his first house in 1946, and for over fifty years he has continued to make a significant contribution to the architectural culture on the West Coast of Canada. He is considered one of the most highly acclaimed architects of his generation, and one of a handful of innovative practitioners responsible for generating the "West Coast Style." Hollingsworth embraced the modern ideals of the mid-century, and continues to design innovative houses to this day.

Fred Thornton Hollingsworth exemplifies an often-unrecognized attribute of the Modern Movement in architecture: the dynamic interplay of placeless-ness with placeful-ness. Fred Hollingsworth has made a remarkable contribution to the modern domestic idiom, being among the most distinguished West Coast practitioners of spatial organization and structural articulation intended to nurture the identity of person with that of the location of domicile. What is more, his architectural legacy, including institutional and commercial design, spans affordable high-quality design and exquisite formal celebration of the art of daily living and dwelling in place.

Modernist architecture came to public prominence from the mid-1920s mainly through photographs of expensive single family houses that were as attuned to their physical setting as to the contemporary avant garde and advanced building technology. The houses of Le Corbusier, Mies van der Rohe and Richard Neutra, or, locally, Peter Thornton and C.B.K. Van Norman, while regarded by their designers as types for comprehensive urban renewal and progressive public architecture, became the central mode of professional and popular discussion. A celebrated example is "Falling Water," the house literally designed into the rural landscape outside Pittsburgh by Frank Lloyd Wright, one of Hollingsworth's chosen mentors. Just as "Falling Water" re-established Wright's reputation and re-asserted his architectonic innovation, so the Modern Movement attained broad aesthetic dominance largely through domestic architecture. Arguably, its greatest legacy (and initial recuperation from revisionist tendencies most frequently termed Postmodernism), occurred in the domestic typology. In turn that typology exerted its most liberalizing and populist congruence in the blue-collar and the white-collar suburbs. Fred Hollingsworth's particular contribution is a succession of attractive houses exemplified by the single-story wood frame Neoteric type built for Robert Hill in 1951 (published in Canadian Homes and Gardens in August 1952 as "a big house living on a small-house budget") or by those repeat commissions for the Moon (1950 and 1979) and Trethewey (1960 and 1987) families. Each was as economical as they were appropriate to both lifestyle and setting through a sophisticated simplicity of plan and structure matched by subtlety of formal articulation and detailing.

The Movement, as its progenitors preferred to call their new attitude to design and society, endeavoured to devise places of habitation, work and recreation that embodied universal values and local conditions. They rejected the preoccupation with style because it confused superficial appearance with structural integrity and privileged historical example over contemporary need. That preoccupation with style had too often resulted in the pastiche of monuments of defunct or deficient social order. Above all they sought to redirect industrial technology toward the provision of better environment and healthier lifestyles to the widest number of people. Thus the original idea — set of Modernism — coalesced and charged in reaction to the social disparity but technical opportunity revealed by the First World War — enshrined comprehensive change. The Modernist's exemplar was no longer either scholar artist, or craftsperson designer, but the pragmatic problem-solving engineer. They contended that engagement with questions of function and material performance actually disclosed true aesthetic. The engineer was the hero of Le Corbusier's seminal text of Modernism, *Vers un architecture*, first published in 1923 and translated into English as *Towards a New Architecture* in 1927. According to Le Corbusier, engineer architects had invented the greatest standard type of building, the ancient Greek temple. He believed that the engineer's analytic could speed reconstruction of war-damaged and ethically decrepit western Europe. Additionally he allied it with the redirection of western technology and ideology away from suppressive internal and imperial regulation towards the realization of a universal and egalitarian Radiant City or Green City. Those utopian projects by Le Corbusier expanded on the social housing built in Weimar Germany by Ernst May or Walter Gropius, founder of the celebrated Bauhaus school of architecture and design. From those imaginary and real places could emerge

Opposite page: Robert Hill house

paradigms of better place and community for everyone everywhere, whether in tropical Africa or the diverse climates and geographies of Canada.

Le Corbusier linked this radical vision to the agency of aeronautical technology which alike fascinated Hollingsworth. In 1935 Le Corbusier published a book in English entitled *Aircraft*. The aphoristic text, more reminiscent of William Blake's impassioned poetry than intellectual argument, was illustrated by beguiling photographs of aircraft, aero engines and the experience of flying. From the sky, Le Corbusier contended, the failings of modern urbanism were both more apparent and capable of rectification so as to build better community. Hollingsworth came to architecture from a brief apprenticeship in sheet metal work and developing wartime production

Moon house

illustration at the Boeing plant on Sea Island in Vancouver, drafting diagrams to explain the assembly of complex aircraft components. This gave him a fascination with the geometry of functional form and with the interplay between individual elements and complicated systems. An early statement of that adroit combination came in the cost-effective organization of four living units at the intersection of two cross-axial concrete blocks for the Shalal Gardens quadriplex in North Vancouver completed in 1950. A later statement is the compact but rhythmically composed Smith house carved into a confined plot replete with a swimming pool in West Vancouver of 1990. A champion model aircraft maker to this day, he also obtained a pilot's license, thereby expanding the parameters of his artistic and architectural production.

Though born in Britain, he grew up in Vancouver during the Depression and experienced the socially divisive economic and political conditions that Modernism sought to alleviate. He experienced the events and socio-cultural forces that made the ideas and imagery of Modernism relevant and welcome. He has designed buildings that have invested singular meaning in natural place while creating spaces of sophisticated sociability. His design achievement is remarkable for its elevated yet pragmatic sense of the place of architecture in society.

Top: Shalal Gardens
Bottom: Smith house

## Locating Hollingsworth

HOLLINGSWORTH'S BELIEF IN THE CONJOINED DEMOCRATIC AND AESTHETIC ROLES OF ARCHITECTURE reflected the new vision of architectural agency argued by the Modernists. He also respected the efficacy of their new functionalist diagnostic of the architectural problem. Their assertion that abstract and analytic form could convey the sensual and spiritual also resonated with his musicianship. An accomplished tenor saxophonist, he led a successful band, Fred Thornton Hollingsworth and his Orchestra. They performed at venues around the Lower Mainland and on C.B.C. radio after he left Boeing and, briefly worked in 1946 as a commercial artist. His earnings enabled him to purchase a lot in Capilano Highlands and build a family house that became the main site of his practice and remains his domicile. The delight he had in experimenting with music, especially jazz, thus became the means by which he started architectural practice. That transition happened through a regulation imposed by the developer of Capilano Highlands. This was his friend Eric Allan, who liked jazz and whose wartime service convinced him of the commercial potential of new modes of housing design and lifestyle. Allan had engaged as design consultant the respected and forward-looking Vancouver architectural firm of Sharp and Thompson. The original partners designed in the Edwardian eclectic style; Neo-Classical for the Vancouver Club (1907), Neo-Gothic for the University of British Columbia (from 1913), or Arts and Crafts for high-end housing. By 1945 Charles Thompson assumed direction and brought into partnership two younger University of Toronto-trained architects, Charles "Ned" Pratt and R.A.D. "Bob" Berwick. Each admired the uncompromising geometrical and structural expression of purpose in transatlantic Modernist design, popularly, if erroneously, designed as the "International Style". Ned Pratt inspected Hollingsworth's drawings and was so impressed by Fred's grasp of the congruence of functioning space, plan, construction and visual effect that he immediately persuaded Thompson to make a job offer.

From the outset Hollingsworth was able to imagine and create a physical setting for what Michel de Certeau in *The Practice of Everyday Life* (English text 1984) has described as the "signifying practices" of individual placement. Hollingsworth's appreciation of clients' sense of and search for personal spatialization derived from close analysis of their preferences and aspirations. That he translated into built form through his understanding of the communicative language of planning and design. Besides innate drafting ability, he had extended his expertise in the visualization of complicated formal-spatial connections at the Vancouver School of Art. Among his teachers was Bert Binning and among his peers, Ronald Thom, who also developed a comparable talent for making highly satisfying and functional spatial sequences from simple compositional components. Binning's witty drawings of daily events and abstract contemporary pictures indicate how Hollingsworth and Thom were initiated into the subtleties inherent within in carefully considered two-dimensional delineation that concentrates means while expanding effects. Furthermore, Binning regarded art-making as essential to community, artistic values as necessary to the built environment, and social activism as the responsibility of the artist; he even dabbled in architecture, designing his own Vancouver house (of sufficient architectural means to be the first West Coast building listed on the National Register of Historic Buildings).

Binning was a leading figure in the highly influential Art in Living Group whose legacy Hollingsworth respected. Its members mounted three major interventions on the Vancouver social and cultural scene. The most important was their 1944 "New Community" scheme for comprehensively reconstructing the blighted downtown east Strathcona district. The decrepit wooden housing was to be replaced by a landscaped housing development that combined the main features of contemporary European, British and American town planning: the rationalist garden cities Le Corbusier promoted through the Congrés internationaux de l'architecture moderne [CIAM] and the more dispersed Neighbourhood Unit paradigm favoured in Britain and the United States. Those planning solutions had been synthesized in proposals for rebuilding London drawn up by the Modern Architecture Research Group [MARS], the British wing of CIAM. Amongst its members was Fred Lasserre who had trained at the University of Toronto School of Architecture with Pratt and Berwick. Lasserre was brought to Vancouver in 1946 to establish a Department of Architecture at U.B.C. There Hollingsworth would both complete training under the mentorship of two of the School's best faculty, John Peeps and Wolfgang Gerson, and latterly teach part-time. Hollingsworth admired Lasserre's acumen and his wish to bring radical international practice to bear on regional design issues. But he chaffed at Lasserre's stress on cognitive over intuitive criteria and tendency to conventionalized teaching, including a disinclination to alleviate gender disparity. Nevertheless, under Lasserre's directorship the provincial architectural profession prospered in terms of repute. A distinct West Coast regional idiom in both institutional and residential building won national renown and international recognition.

Hollingsworth deepened his passion for practical yet refined architecture in the offices of what had now become Sharp Thompson Berwick and Pratt. He and Thom were allowed considerable latitude in completing the firm's residential commissions including the housing component of the initially innovative and comprehensive new town begun in 1952 at Kitimat in northern B.C. for the Alcan Corporation. The expanding demography and economy of post-war Canada and British Columbia supported a remarkable extension of architect-designed housing. Hollingsworth's clients continued to be young professionals, many of whom had become used to higher technical standards during their war service, from ergonomic spatial organization to technological equipment. The exigencies of war, including vicious ethno-racial genocide, had instilled a yearning for stable society founded in a nostalgic reconsideration of familial home — one that coincidentally presented enormous opportunity for the redirection of wartime manufacture into consumer goods and appliances. The confluence of essentially disparate political values and social objectives is manifest in the establishment in 1947 of the Central [later Canada] Mortgage and Housing Corporation. On the one hand C.M.H.C. operated to advantage entrepreneurial property development and individual house ownership, on the other it enacted a notable range and quality of housing schemes to benefit the economically or socially disadvantaged across Canada. Their focus was affordable housing. The Corporation thus demonstrated how radical policy often operates through conservative structures. That combination also existed in the vein of Modernist practice that influenced Hollingsworth and the development of North American

Modernism. Between 1952 and 1958 Hollingsworth entered partnership with William Birmingham — initially as associate while awaiting his final accreditation with the Architectural Institute of B.C. They collaborated on commercial and institutional projects in the Vancouver region and northern province while continuing individual house practices.

THE SITING OF SCIENTIFIC AND AESTHETIC IDEAS OF NEW SOCIETY AND DESIGN IN THE HOUSE PRE-DATE ## Defining Modernism

the Modern Movement. The fifteenth-century Italian artist architect and theorist L.B. Alberti, had, for one, likened the house to a small city. Le Corbusier mechanized the analogy by stressing that city and house alike should be conceived as machines and mechanisms. He meant, as most contemporaries and Hollingsworth realized, that the domestic functions could be best comprehended in terms of the processes of living, a growing proportion of which were mechanical. One aspect was Hollingsworth's (and other's) collaboration with the B.C. lumber industry on the manufacture of standardized pre-cut structural units. The main product was the Silverwall plywood panel that had an eight foot module. Silverwall reflected Hollingsworth's awareness of the limitations of fully manufactured pre-fabrication systems tried by Buckminster Fuller, Walter Gropius, or Le Corbusier. Hollingsworth recognized the difficulties of delivery and location, together with the resistance of the building industry and average consumer. He preferred the partial and variable system Frank Lloyd Wright enacted in his Usonian post-and-beam houses, and the warmth and versatility of the wood as a material. He also concurred with William Dudok's acknowledgement of the interdependent nature of design. An avid reader of international architectural journals Hollingsworth quite likely was aware of the precepts expounded in a lecture delivered at the Architectural Association in London in June 1934:

"Whatever changes may take place in our day, architecture still is, and always will continue to be, the art of creating spaces, spaces which will have to come up to the requirements of our ever varying and changing life. Logical and sound construction of the space-enclosure is the means to this; a very pregnant means it is true, but never the end. Good construction in itself does not necessarily lead to architectural beauty, and I don't see why the technical compositions should always have to be externally perceptible."

The passage was reprinted in one of the books that entrenched Modernism in the architectural schools. Written in 1940 by the British architect Julian Leathart and entitled *Style in Architecture*, it reinforced the main texts: Le Corbusier's *Towards a New Architecture*; J.M. Richard's *Modern Architecture, an Introduction* published by Penguin Books in 1941 and almost immediately reprinted in paperback; Walter Gropius's *The New Architecture and the Bauhaus*, 1935, the English version of his original German text of 1933; Siegfried Giedion's *Space Time and Architecture*, 1941; and Jean-Louis Sert's *Can Our Cities Survive?* 1944. (The last two books owed much to the efforts, respectively as translator and compiler, of the British planning educator Jaqueline Tyrwhitt who acted as Secretary of the war-dispersed CIAM and organized its enormously important 1947 and 1952 conferences at Bridgewater and Hoddesdon U.K. while lecturing at the University of Toronto).

The particular interest of Leathart's book, in addition to its long print-run, was its normalizing of the radical intention of Modernism and relation of the Movement to the profoundly altered post 1945 geo-political and social environment. Leathart usefully summarized the transformations wrought by Modernism: the rejection of stylism; the recovery of an effective integration of contemporary capacity and traditional value; the dependence of aesthetic on a "process of ordered functional expression," and the embrace of mobility and systems, surmounting the once draconian authority of space and time directed towards the attainment of equitarian social order. Leathart also voiced the reconstituted religious and moral dynamic, however naïve in retrospect, embedded in the Modern Movement. This dynamic would confound the "financial and economic inco-herency in which greed, fear and ruthlessness combine to oppress the virtuous and the wicked alike." This is not to present Leathart as either a major inspiration upon Hollingsworth or the ideation of post-war Modernism. Somewhat to the contrary, since the proliferation of architectural and planning schools in Reconstruction-era North America and Europe quickly enjoined conventionalized pedagogy. At U.B.C. this moved between successive allegiance to a supposedly Corbusian and Miesian construct interspersed by periodic reference to Gropius, Lloyd Wright and the Pacific Coast Modernists (from California, Oregon and Washington States). Leathart's book demonstrates the professional and more broadly popular acceptance of change on a com-prehensive scale and at an ethical level. Of especial significance is his championing of the idea of transcendence. This involved the overcoming of the geographical and societal division so apparent during the Second World War and its immediate aftermath of both imperial collapse and Cold War conflict. Similarly it involved the formulation of place as inclusionary instead of exclusionary, an idea literally expressed in the window-wall of the West Coast Modernist idiom Hollingsworth helped create. Lastly it involved the re-consideration of individuality as in the embrace of social collectivity and connectivity — the subsequent decline of which is manifest in the enclosure of the open landscaping favoured by the West Coast Modernists. The vision of equitable community, collaborative humanity, and higher societal purpose for architecture — all ideals that inform Hollingsworth's work — are implied in Leathart's phrase, "All architectural styles tend to decline when the objective of personal taste is imposed as an end in itself."

## Modernist Representation

THE ASPIRATION FOR A REGENERATIVE ARCHITECTURAL CULTURE IS EQUALLY EVIDENT IN THE INCISIVE monochrome photographs illustrating Leathart's text. They reflect the emergence from the 1930s of highly sophisticated architectural photography that in its apparent straightforwardness caught the tenor of emergent transatlantic Modernism. An early triumph in public esteem was the display of photographs of new functionalist building across Europe in the exhibition of "International Style Architecture" originally installed at the New York Museum of Modern Art in 1932. The organizers, the historian H.R. Hitchcock and the critic, later architect Philip Johnson, used the photographic medium and the new techniques enabled by recent camera and lens development to assert a complement of architectonic effects not always representative of architectural practice. Thereafter the main professional journals — *Architectural Record*, *L'Architecture d'aujourd'hui*, *Architectural Review* and *Journal of the Royal Architectural Institute of Canada* or, locally, *Western Homes and Living* — engaged the most adept photographers of the built form. They were the technical peers of both the journalistic and the art photographers, who were altering the discourse of visual culture. The constrained focal and light range plus the black and white print of contemporary photography suited the emphasis in Modernist architecture on geo-metrical massing, planal composition, space modulation, functional expression and abstract — non-historical or associational — articulation. The monochrome medium even enhanced the more patterned and textured surfaces preferred by craft exponents such as Wright, Harwell Harris in California or John Yeon in Oregon. The combination of linear definition and tonal interplay in the photographs of, say, John Yerbury in Britain, Julius Shulman in California, or Otto Landauer, Graham Warrington and Selwyn Pullan in Vancouver, resulted in remarkable formal logic and authenticity. Such talented photographers could intensify the rationality of structure and psychological force of space and light as well as the marriage of building to sur-rounding. And they almost always succeeded in simultaneously depicting the subject building's architectural currency and distinctiveness.

Pullan Studio

Hollingsworth befriended several of the local architectural photographers. He shared their aesthetic objectives of keener visualization of reality and mobilization of visual modes of communication. In 1962 he designed for Selwyn Pullan a new photographic studio attached to his existing house. The simple but bold concrete and wood structure together with the ample glazing, engage its steeply wooded North Shore setting. The ordering presence of the studio in the landscape also signified the re-ordering of external and internal space that both Hollingsworth and Pullan practiced with the objective of reinforcing their respective properties.

THE WEST COAST "RENAISSANCE" AND "WEST COAST STYLE" BECAME WIDELY ACKNOWLEDGED AS cultural entities through the agency of the local architectural photographers and their publications for public consumption. Their images transported the innovations in place-making architecture at the western margin of Canada to the places of distributive cultural authority — initially Montreal, then Toronto, and subsequently even to New York and London. They rendered the places of West Coast Modernism familiar to those engaged in devising or valuing the qualities of modern living. This spatial interchange of place tended to heighten aesthetic alliance while celebrating its differentiated expression. That process, however, would augment the devolution of Modernist motive into formal uniformity and materialist rather than communitarian enterprise. Modernism became allied with the paraphernalia of the fast growing consumer sector fuelled by the buoyant post-war economy and frequently imbricated in architectural photography. The aestheticized popular consumerism that prospered alongside the idealistic egalitarianism of the Modern Movement, is exemplified in an advertisement for aluminum doors from the March 1959 issue of *The Canadian Architect*. It depicts a glamorous young woman attired in a stylish fur coat and

### West Coast Modernism

high heels stepping through the door of a Modernist office tower. Ironically the visual triggers of persuasive meaning ally conventional Modernist design with the inversion of its original socialist concept of industrial technology and gender politics. Sexual object, rather than subject of social reformation, her purpose is to reiterate stereotypes of Modernist artefact. Similarly, contemporary architectural publicity reverted to older syndromes, that valorized single building and individual architect.

The Modernist reform of architecture Hollingsworth and his peers implemented on the West Coast inevitably became subject to the diverse forces determining later modern society. Nevertheless those forces and the architects' interpretation of Modernist tenet and practice — more diverse than unitary from the outset — resulted in new socio-cultural practice that mediated the imposed with the wanted order of things. For as Hollingsworth realized from his heuristic training in, and all-embracing appreciation of Modern Movement design, the practice of architecture is always multivalent and contingent. It is about placing spaces in places that are as changing as unchanging, and under spatial conditions that are equally transient due to the temporalities of human existence, preference and circumstance.

Modernist Discourses HOLLINGSWORTH TEMPERED PRAGMATISM WITH IMAGINATIVE AND THEORETICAL INQUIRY. HE HELPED erect his own house and those of friends in replication of Gropius's Bauhaus pedagogy of learning by doing. His processes and results were often intuitive. But he also traveled to meet and talk with architects he judged exemplary, on several occasions venturing forth in his Morris Minor, the veritable British peoples' automobile and signifier of Modernist affirmation of both standardization and individual mobility. In 1951 he drove across the northern United States —

Neoteric House

before the Trans-Canada highway and jet travel reinforced the geography of confederation — to explore training with Wright. Once at Wright's Taliesin East in Wisconsin he discovered the master reclining in a deck chair, tanning; during their ensuing conversation Fred also discovered an authoritarianism at odds with the organic subtlety of Wright's architecture. Subsequently he journeyed to Chicago to meet one of Wright's anathema, Mies van der Rohe, puzzling at the contrast between the German's lyrical metamorphosis of dimensional and structural system and his insistence that students learn through mundane repetitive exercise. Through Binning he had already met Richard Neutra who was less preoccupied with monumental architectonic statement. Neutra, like Hollingsworth, was more concerned with designing the domestic scene as generative locus for community. He returned to California to renew acquaintance with Neutra and make contact with other luminaries of deign. These ranged from Erich Mendelsohn, the most humanistic of all the German Modernists, to Harwell Harris, the scion of craft Modernism, Bernard Maybeck, the rogue practitioner of an architecture that encompassed the Beaux Arts, Arts and Crafts and proto Post-Modernist, and to Buckminster Fuller, the architect of advanced technological innovation in urban development and system. Hollingsworth first interviewed Maybeck under a favourite oak tree in his San Francisco garden, continuing to admire Maybeck's unconventional attitude to architectural composition and construction. Fred avowed recently that he was "really a Maybeckian." By contrast, he valued the anti-idiosyncratic and locally embedded design modes of two contemporary Pacific Northwest architects, Pietro Belluschi, and Paul Thiry. Their architecture regionalized the universalist principles of Modernism. They transposed its metal and concrete paradigm into a wooden vernacular that embraced the coastal landscape and climate through traditional and modern construction, orientation and the use of extensive glazing. Hollingsworth's empathy for organic naturalist interpretation of Modernism would be confirmed by the consistent relation of his houses and buildings to specific location and setting.

HOLLINGSWORTH DEFINED A STRATEGY OF PRACTICE FROM EXPLORATIONS OF CONCEPTUAL AND ACTUAL place. He anchored the strategy to Frank Lloyd Wright's synthesis of European Arts and Crafts with Asian aesthetic in satisfaction of American requirement. But Hollingsworth was neither captive to one paradigm nor dogmatic. He enjoyed the stimulus of discussion with colleagues who, like his friend Douglas Simpson, espoused more abstract disciplinary notions of form and technique. He also gathered a group of peers, informally named "The Intellects" and included Ron Thom, Barry Downs (his partner 1963-68), Arthur Erickson, Beans Justice, and Woodruff "Bud" Wood. They together valued the honouring of contextual qualities but exercised distinct architectural authority. To those ends and out of respect for both Wright and Maybeck, Hollingsworth called his strategy organic.

## Hollingsworth's Design Strategy

What did his organic Modernism comprise? He defined it around seven principles of design approach and execution which he considered to be already apparent in the house built at Edmonton in 1951 for Dr. William Shandro:

1) *the use of locally produced materials including naturally derived components,*
2) *the adaptation of natural structural devices such as the cantilever,*
3) *the alliance of built to topographical form, using orientation to gain vista and environmental efficiency,*
4) *the active inter-connection of interior volume to external setting,*
5) *the free spatial interchange between defined areas of communal and personal activity,*
6) *the integral expression of structure in form and aesthetic effect,*
7) *the exploitation of the space-making and space-expanding properties of the interplay of plane and geometry.*

The purport of those principles are summarized in two sentences Hollingsworth coined to describe his design concept and execution: "Good architecture comes from being essential" and "Architecture should be of site not on it."

In company with Ned Pratt, whose mental geography of Modernism was equally international and who wrote the first definition of West Coast Modernism, Hollingsworth saw local conditions as the main function to be accommodated by specific buildings. The maritime geography of the Lower Mainland, wooded and often steep in North and West Vancouver, invigorated the planar vocabulary of Modernism. Modernist preference for modular construction — the post-and-beam system was well established in 1930s British and European practice — suited the abundant local supplies of wood which were improved from the late 1940s by kiln drying and standardized cutting. In turn these initiated new products such as plywood and Gluelam beams. Modernist functionalism also matched the relative consensus on spatial and service requirements of all income groups consequent upon the buoyant post-war economy and advent of mass consumerism and media. Hollingsworth responded to the post-war Vancouver geographical and socio-cultural environment with a series of variable generic house designs carrying such brand names as Neoteric or Flying Arrow. Even the advent of wealthier clients and Neo-Liberal social values from the 1970s did not interrupt either his environmental ethos or his functional organicism. He did, however, augment the compositional sophistication of his designs with increasingly choice site plots, exploring the material quality and visual subtlety of his articulation. In his later houses he also endeavoured to pursue and satisfy more fully, the psychology of habitation — especially the conjoined desire for repose/stimulus, familiarity/changefulness, privacy/conviviality — through the realization of personal and familial hierarchies of space, transparency of visual incident, and sensory value. He became successively adept at exploiting the qualities of northern Pacific light, sometimes pellucid and subdued, always modifying mass and modulating surface.

## In Practice

HOLLINGSWORTH APPLIED HIS SEVEN PRINCIPLES TO BOTH INSTITUTIONAL AND COMMERCIAL COMMISSIONS. At Eric Allan's behest, he built the earliest A-frame church in the region, St. Catherine's Anglican Church in the Capilano Highlands Subdivision (1948). The transition from domestic to institutional scale was even easier in an innovative 1961 scheme for Berkeley Private [Retirement] Hospital at White Rock, south of Vancouver. In place of the hospital ward model, he created a series of independent quarters for married or single people. Integrated with service and recreation accommodation, those units included balcony gardens. Thereby, each resident could maintain a good level of autonomous activity and identity while being under protective monitoring and/or medical care. His schemes for apartment buildings in the boom following the repeal in 1956 of the by-laws limiting height in Vancouver's West End, avoided the utilitarian finish and repetitive iconography of those built. He adapted the strong massing, inventive but tight planning and structural geometries of Frank Lloyd Wright's Price Tower at Bartlesville in Ohio (for which he had been invited to undertake the working drawings when visiting Wright in 1951). Hollingsworth had the ability to ally visual delight and intellectual interest with the provision of purposeful and economic buildings. To that end he experimented with repetitive angled modules, as for the hexagonal showroom he designed for a gas company in Surrey, 1954. Such competency was especially evident in two now demolished offices in Vancouver. The social mission and urban presence of the Red Feather Community and Chest Council 1953-54, predecessor to the United Way Campaign, were cleverly reinforced by Hollingsworth's exploitation of a sloping site to create an impressive three-story window wall on the entrance façade, augmented visually by projected eaves and angled staircase projections at each end. For Allied Heat and Fuel Limited (1962-63)

Berkeley Hospital

UBC Faculty of Law Building

he studded the concrete-block walls with coal, provided wheel chair access and integrated the offices with the central public area spanned by exposed laminated cedar beams.

The imagining of user need and preference were integral to his resolution of technical requirements with the generation of aesthetic character. For Hollingsworth, certainly aware of Bruno Taut's 1929 claim of the essential relationship between function and aesthetic, the total architectural effect should have a determinant logic. That appreciation of harmonious diversity Hollingsworth recognized in Asian architecture and landscaping, as well as in Wrightian and Bay Region design. The Imperial Inn Motel in Victoria (1962) indeed pioneered a resurgence of interest in Japanese art and architecture on the West Coast. The public and private accommodation was more closely related in layout, reference to external landscaping and internal spatial organization. The Inn coincided with his planning of a major extension to the Law School at the University of British Columbia (1962-63). He contrasted the bare concrete and glass original building with a low profile, powerfully massed, rectangular complex. The administration, faculty, teaching and library facilities were organized around an L-shaped central courtyard, mostly enclosed and linked to the single circulation corridor. His aim was to rectify the habitual separation of faculty from student and dislocation of individual from communal learning. The Law School retains its unostentatious presence on the much enlarged campus through Hollingsworth's interrelation of layout, circulation and usage with structural form. This bond included an architectonically neat if not universally welcome system, of raised fenestration intended to reduce internal distraction and external observation. The load-bearing work of the wall and the regulatory power of the law — once the modality of colonization but currently of reconstituting the political and property rights of indigenous peoples in B.C. — are symbolized in the horizontally and vertically striated textural concrete fabric framed by smooth mouldings and ornamented by Hollingsworth's recessed square insignia.

In these pages: Robert Hill house

HOLLINGSWORTH OFTEN INCLUDED A VERSION OF THIS MOTIF IN HIS DOMESTIC ARCHITECTURE TO SIGNAL his place among the ancient fraternity of mason builders. But his command of the directive and communicative properties of the processes involved in, and effects resulting from, architectural construction, also corresponds with the complex analytic of 20th-century theory and practice. From the outset of his career Hollingsworth has invested significance and meaning into the commonplace spaces of living. One example is Hollingsworth's unpretentious Robert Hill House (1951), one of several "Flying Arrow" homes built in the Capilano Highlands subdivision. The economical concrete pad with embedded heating coils, wood post-and-beam frame, central

## Accommodating the Modern Family

concrete block chimney, internal plywood paneling and furniture, both built-in and freestanding, created individualized dwelling from standardized component. Although named for the husband — betraying a male gender bias in Modernism at odds with its attention to female requirement and participation — the house enacted the remarkable mixing of progressive with conservative, communal with private interests during the post-1945 decades. The single family home became a vital locus of political and cultural interaction. Bob Hill was mortgage manager for Sun Life Insurance and thereby representative of the coalition around consumerism brokered between corporate capital and democratic socialism. At this sometimes still conflictual intersection of interests and intentions the Modernist project achieved its widest enduring popular acceptance as against its other objectives of comprehensive urban redevelopment and low-cost housing.

The series of photographs Selwyn Pullan took of the Robert Hill house demonstrate Hollingsworth's intuitive grasp of those profound factors of mentality and society explored most fully in Continental Theory. The photographs show spatial environments and affects that evoke Martin Heidegger's concept of dwelling as a conscious living in defined place and exemplify Michel de Certeau's assertion that "space is a practiced place." Despite the obvious newness of the structure, the house occupies rather than intrudes upon its site. Its modest size and uncomplicated yet varied composition engage with the still treed plot and forested mountain scenery. The night-time photograph especially demonstrates Hollingsworth's realization of the protective and communal properties of shelter. A further dimension of the provision of secure and sustaining place within the larger spaces of existence is demonstrated in the photograph of

Hill's daughters playing in the built-in sand pit. The pit was slotted neatly into the intersection of two parts of the concrete slab, adjacent to and overlooked by the kitchen and dining-living room. In the daily rhetoric of the Cold War era the kitchen was the command centre of the social scientific house, contributing by positive and negative processes to emergent gender and economic politics that ultimately enhanced the position of women; indicative of such significant changes occurring in these apparently straightforward spaces, the kitchen became an epitome of the clash between capitalist and communist legitimacy, signified by the 1959 "Kitchen Debate" between Nixon and Kruschev.

All images in these pages: Robert Hill house

In the Hill house the shiny surfaces of new labour-saving appliances and fixtures in the amply-lit kitchen are played against the exposed graining of the wooden cupboards with the effect of enlarging the apparent size of its compressed ergonomic layout. The butted glass windows illuminate food preparation and allow views of playing children, and neighbours, while being protected from glare and rain by deep eaves. The ploy energizes the usually dull right angled corners of other rooms, specifically enabling the insertion of a desk-cum-vanity in the main bedroom. Hollingsworth mobilized a triangular motif to cohere the spatial differentiation (rather than partition) of the interior spaces utilizing inexpensive custom-built furniture. For example, the angled corner of the dining table points into the living room toward the corner fireplace, while simultaneously deflecting the eye respectively to the kitchen and glazed wall to the garden. The fireplace establishes the mythic center of the now less formal, nuclear family. Its prominence is authorized by a serviceable bench seat, book shelves and lighting fixtures. Through such adroit means Hollingsworth managed an extraordinary level of volumetric, textural and aesthetic expression with the hearth as its centerpiece.

**A Modernist Career**   HOLLINGSWORTH'S ARCHITECTURAL ALCHEMY WAS AS VARIED AS IT WAS CONSISTENT IN QUALITY. THOSE qualities are particularly evident in the series of houses he designed at quite different sites for single clients such as Moon (1950, North Vancouver and 1971, Calgary) or Trethewey (1960, Abbotsford and 1987, Haney) or in the comparison between his modest suburban and later expensive waterfront houses in Vancouver, West Vancouver and White Rock. Whereas the curving form and expressed structural frame of the Maltby House in West Vancouver (1964, awarded the Massey Gold for Architecture) differs from the axial on grade arrangement of the Malmgren House in Burnaby (1998-88), the spatialization of client lifestyle is comparably perceptive and effective. The ingeniously contracted formal invention of the Sky Bungalow (1949) resonates in the expansive and artistic manipulation of volume structure and surface in the last house he designed before retiring from practice in 2001. In place of the tight angularity of his early demonstration house erected on the parking lot of the downtown Hudson Bay Department Store, the Kassam House (1999-2002) is anchored onto a large sloping plot above Spanish Banks overlooking English Bay and the North Shore. A gracious geometry of curved and rectangular living and entertaining spaces are marshaled in a sequence that captures patterns of use in relation to the beguiling scenery. Hollingsworth's other late masterworks, the Fluckiger House in White Rock (1988-94), and Bosa House in West Vancouver (1991-93), transform the provision of comprehensive domestic function to a harmonious synthesis of architectural modelling and ornamental composition with their superb waterfront settings.

Maltby house

THE DISTINCTION OF HOLLINGSWORTH'S ARCHITECTURE IS MATCHED BY THE DISTINCTIVENESS OF HIS CAREER. **Hollingsworth Today**
He has attained the highest professional honours while eschewing a high profile practice. He was elected Honorary Fellow of the American Institute of Architect in 1976 after being elected President of the Architectural Institute of British Columbia (1971-72) and of the Royal Architectural Institute of Canada (1975-76). He sustained excellence in middle class housing, that field of the built environment where, by the mid-1960s architects exerted minimal influence. Besides amicable and productive partnerships with Bill Birmingham and Barry Downs, Hollingsworth established an enduringly successful domestic practice. He has never wanted for substantive commissions. All have been derived from unsolicited or repeat patronage. His practice was appropriately located in the attractive additional studio space he built into his original family house, itself a microcosm of his design strategy, craft work and Modernist aesthetic. Convenient yet spacious, homogeneous yet multivalent, the interiors contain examples of his furniture, watercolors and models, together with his appreciation of transatlantic, Asian and aboriginal design. Hollingsworth and Birmingham were indeed among the vanguard of those who comprehended the aesthetic quality of indigenous art; they helped finance the first museum devoted to West Coast First Nations art at Prince Rupert for which Hollingsworth designed a wooden stepped beam structure inspired by North West Coast aboriginal building (1956).

No less significantly, Hollingsworth brought high Modernist architectural culture, exemplified by the Case Study houses published in *Art and Architecture*, into the realm of ordinary suburban living. That realm, notwithstanding its disjunction from the utopic myth of popular advertising media, has proven a remarkably robust socio-cultural invention; and the economical houses of the Modernist remain a more sustainable solution for the endemic preference for individual home ownership than those built from the late 1980s. Above all Hollingsworth created visually memorable and stimulating architecture that served wider social need and particular individual aspiration. Even when completing his later high cost commissions, Hollingsworth devised a series of economical courtyard "Enviromatic" houses that exploited orientation, solar panels and vegetation to conserve energy and thereby provide affordable, environmentally responsible domicile. His life's work continues to envigorate, inspirit and enchant the lives of those for whom he designed. Whether domestic or institutional, his architecture asserts regional sensibility and sensitivity to place in the artistic construction of significant and meaningful space. ▪

Select Bibliography

1. a) Rhodri Windsor Liscombe "Organic Modernism: The Architecture of F.T. Hollingsworth," *Journal of the Society for the Study of Architecture in Canada*, 21 (June 1996) 2: 44-50.

   b) *The New Spirit: Modern Architecture in Vancouver 1938-1963* (Montreal/Vancouver: Canadian Centre for Architecture, and Douglas & McIntyre, 1997).

   c) "The Fe-Male Spaces of Modernism: A Western Canadian Perspective," *26 Prospects* (2001): 667-700.

2. Dolores Hayden, *Building Suburbia: Green Fields and Urban Growth 1820-2000,* (New York: Pantheon Books, 2002).

3. Harold Kalman, *A History of Canadian Architecture,* (Toronto: Oxford University Press, 1994).

4. Don Luxton & Associates, *The Modern Architecture of North Vancouver 1930-1965,* (District of North Vancouver, 1997).

5. Sherry McKay, "Western Living Western Homes," *Journal of the Society for the Study of Architecture in Canada*, 4 (September 1989) 3: 65-74.

6. "Western Homes, Western Living Exhibition," Charles H. Scott Gallery, Vancouver B.C. June 9 to July 25, 2003.

# On Organic Architecture

THE "ORGANIC PRINCIPLE" GREW OUT OF THE RAPID GROWTH OF AMERICAN PRAIRIE CITIES. THE SELF-confidence of a prosperous time, along with new industrial techniques, stimulated new ideas and philosophy. Along with the development of the tall buildings, which grew out of this successful business growth period, architects started to examine patterns of living in relation to housing design. Such ideas as a building could be natural as nature itself, took on new meaning. Ideas about such things as "tradition" were re-examined, along with "ornament" and how to re-design it. "Spirit" and how to express it as an emotion, form and function and their relativity, along with many other ideas and questions began to formulate into a new ideal theory of design.

The architects of the times began to see fresh and new opportunities for design and the great early modernist Louis Sullivan gave such questions new answers like the expression "form follows function." While later he stated that "form and function are one," so a whole new approach to planning and design was created.

Along with the idea that nature was a fine example to follow, the "natural house" became a logical answer. New freer floor plans began to appear, relating form and function as an expression of life patterns. The site of the building became a greater concern in that the building should relate to its site, as natural as all other parts of nature. For example, if a slope or hill grade was on the site the building should be set into it and becomes part of it. Hence the saying "of the thing not on it," to become a part of the whole site as if it had grown there also. Large walls of panels of glass were introduced to visually relate the interior spaces to the exterior natural surroundings and plant areas or gardens came inside the rooms. These panels of glass when faced south or

by Fred Thornton Hollingsworth

southwest or east accompanied with large overhanging roofs made solar control possible and the house had changed forever.

Materials themselves became a new way of expression, as did the structure and its covering skin, each could be looked at for its own value, for its own beauty and functional relationship to its use. Wood was often used and left as wood, brick, concrete, stone, glass, metals all had their own beauty and were seen as surfaces that should be expressed and appreciated for their own contribution to the beauty of the building. The structural frame was to become a part of the whole, not necessarily exposed "so as to rattle the skeleton," but to become part of the whole form as in most of nature. Expressed, following the concept "form and function are one," structure and covering skin combine to create form. Further, materials should be allowed to show for themselves the expression "of the thing not on it." This applies to such things as coatings, like paint over wood, brick or concrete. Paint is something "on it" when applied to wood, whereas a stain goes into the wood, leaves the grain visible and becomes part "of the thing." Another example is copper roofing and flashing which does not require painting but ages to its own beautiful color of verdigris green and creates its own protective skin.

"Truth" in architecture is a divinity. So the organic principle has no use for materials of falsity. For example, any material which imitates another's qualities and/or appearance, and does not state its own "truth" are to be rejected. Plastics imitating wood grain panels are a typical example of fake "photographic" use. However, plastic materials, which show and state their own true qualities, have a valid place in use.

"Space" should have a sense of continuity, horizontally and vertically, creating a new sense of freedom, always in scale to the human need and function, with an expression of emotion. Continuity with the interior and exterior as appropriate, with a quality of expression for light and shade in motion. A feeling of open variation with the movement from space to space. Respect for various emotions, moods and feelings.

"Light" and its daily and seasonal movements, are of great concern, as elements of surprise and delight, and are essential to the architect's expression in space relations, (both internal and external). The use of light and shaded spaces create opportunities for qualities of change and an additional sense of beauty.

"Ornament" is an art form of embellishment as old as the art of building itself. Often, generally in the form of "applicate" with little or no connection to the building it is applied to. Some modernists and others reject its use totally. To the organic, "ornament" is an integral element of architecture; it is of a similar nature as a flower to a plant. It is again, "of the thing not on it," if well designed, it will relate to the existing forms, compositions and expressions of the rest of the work. Often a literal part of the building, as much as the structure, skin, or other specific parts. It must be conceived in the same sense as the organic work it becomes part of, to express those terms in poetic detail. Generally such ornament would be cast in the concrete, pressed into the plaster, milled into the wood, lade-up in the brick as a pattern or, for example, formed into a sheet metal facia, or other metals, which all express the phrase "of the thing not on it."

The organic building is intended to be an honest expression of the use it is intended to perform. An honest open expression of its own structure, closure faces or skin. It embraces its site and belongs there. It is a true expression of the materials used to form it and offers comfort and delight to its users. It is never expressive of its past, but offers flexibility to the future. Finally, it is a principle that offers an architecture that is stable and will go forward with time and provide spaces for its users that will age and mellow gracefully. ▣

Early Work 1946-1960

# Hollingsworth 1946/60/79

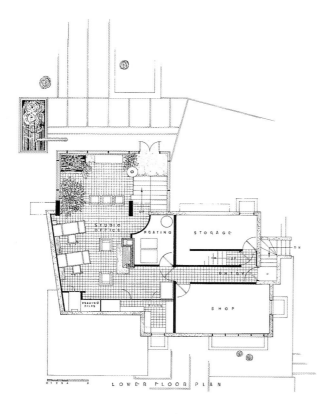

LOWER FLOOR PLAN

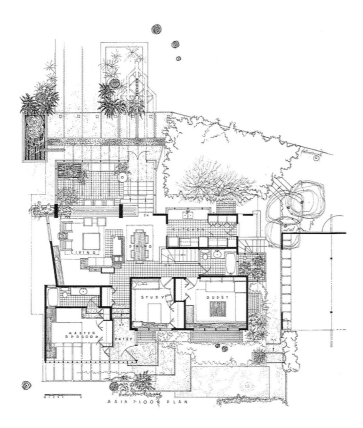

MAIN FLOOR PLAN

Hollingsworth's own house was designed for a lot in the Capilano Highlands development in North Vancouver. The living room and general areas are turned away from the street to face the south and the back garden. First designed to sit on a concrete slab with radiant heat, this had to be altered, as no one in 1946 would give a mortgage without a basement. The house was designed on a 4' module, the width of a standard plywood sheet. Materials were kept to a minimum with cedar plywood used on the interior and cedar siding on the exterior. The interior is an open plan with the living room and dining room separated by the brick fireplace.

In 1960 the entrance porch was converted to an office that allowed clients to come and go without having to enter the rest of the house. A further renovation was done in 1979 when the office and studio were relocated to an atrium space at the back of the house using part of the basement. The atrium looks out onto the back garden and facilitates a flow from the inside to the outside.

# Neoteric 1949

Designed as an economical house for Eric Allen, the developer of the Capilano Highlands, the neoteric houses were a simple post and beam construction that utilized fir beams and inexpensive cedar planking inside and out. The floors were concrete slabs with underflow warm air heating. The open plan featured the living room on the street side and family room on the backside towards the garden. All that separated the kitchen, dining, living and family room was the chimney. The end wall of the living room and family room was a brick cavity wall. The neoteric had a flat roof with a clerestory to bring in light to the interior spaces. The garage was integrated into the roof structure.

A similar house called the Flying Arrow had the living room on a forty-five degree angle and a peaked roof. All the roof trusses were exposed and simple decking on the roof. Like the neoteric these houses utilized fir posts, cedar, brick and concrete slab floors with radiant heating. The houses were designed to fit on any lot in any direction. About fourteen Neoteric and six Flying Arrows were built.

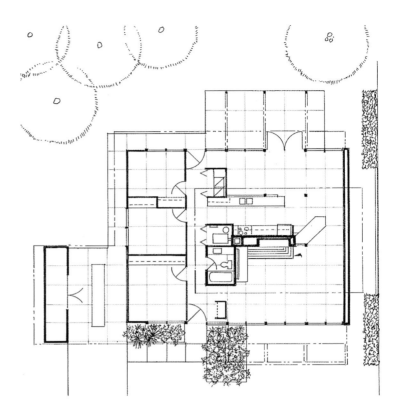

# Sky Bungalow 1949

Designed as a show
house to promote
Capilano Highlands, it
was constructed on the
parking lot of the Hudson's
Bay Department Store.
It was allowed to take up
three parking spaces
only, so the solution was
to elevate the house, one
story off the ground on
two brick structural
columns and a brick
utility room to support
three cantilevered steel
beams. It featured an
open plan, frame
construction with
clerestory windows.

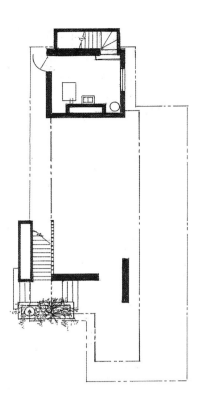

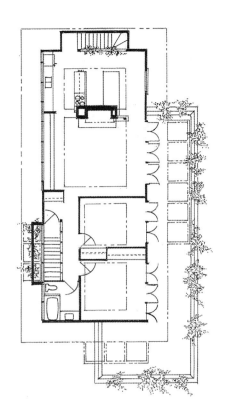

The outside and inside were cedar board and batten. The house had many built-in features including stainless steel counter tops. It not only promoted modern house design, but also furniture and appliances. It was considered startlingly contemporary and introduced many people to what would soon become common features of West Coast houses. The house was sold and moved to a location in the Capilano Highlands

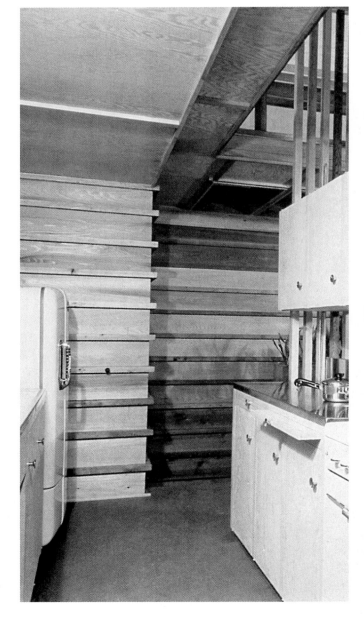

# Moon I 1950

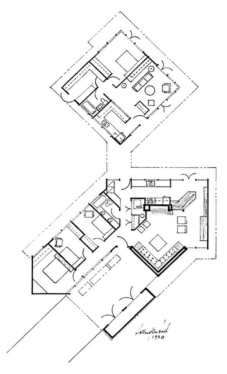

The house is a large Neoteric type post and beam structure turned at a 45-degree angle so it formed a "V" pointed to the street. The asymmetrical layout gives a feeling of flowing from space to space. The house has two structures, one containing the living room, dining room, kitchen and bedrooms and the other a guesthouse, with a garden space between the structures. It sits on a concrete slab with radiant heating. Cedar board and batten were used both inside and out. Cavity brick walls were used with a decorative pattern inset into the brick with sheet plate glass between to separate inside and outside open spaces. As well, there is built-in seating in the living room.

# Capilano Garden Court (Shalal Gardens) 1950

Designed around a cross formation of brick walls, which allowed for four apartments to each structure. These four-plex apartments could be oriented in any direction to take advantage of the sun. The two story apartments had the living room, dining room and kitchen on the main floor and two bedrooms upstairs. The corridor along the bedrooms is wide enough to be used as a sitting area. The space over the living room and dining room is open to the ceiling with a glass wall all the way up on the exterior living room wall. None of the units looked into the other allowing for privacy and each had a small fenced-in garden off the corner of the living room. Plaster finishes were used on the interior walls along with brick, and each unit had a large fireplace. For their time these apartments were considered quite innovative in the use of both horizontal and vertical space.

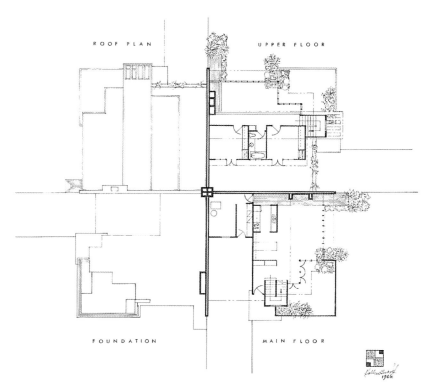

ROOF PLAN          UPPER FLOOR

FOUNDATION          MAIN FLOOR

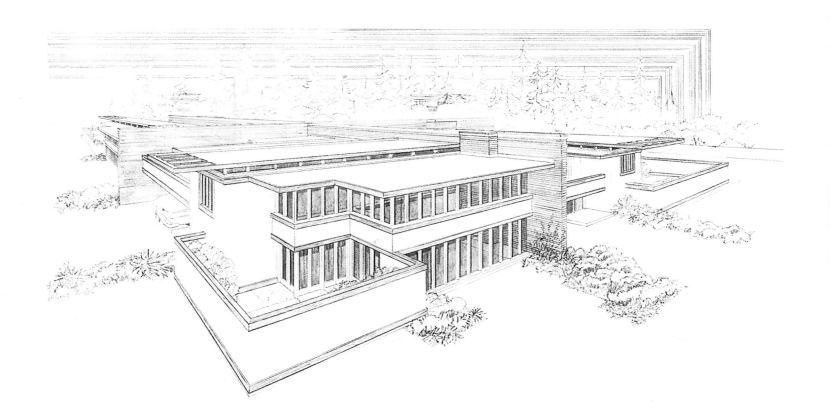

# Red Feather Building (Community Chest) 1950

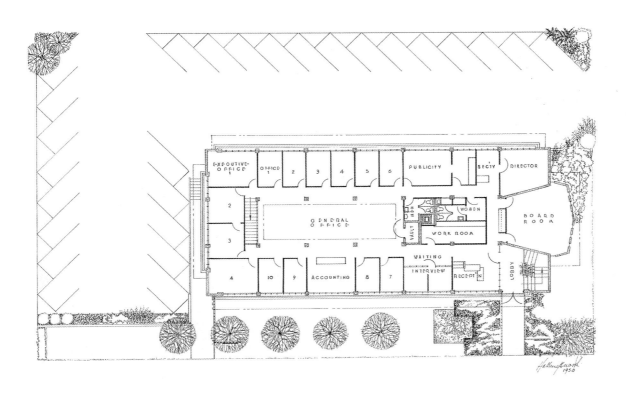

The building is a clean and simple expression of modern design. Constructed of concrete, which flares at the top of the columns. Glass was used extensively and steel window mullions 1/2 inches wide made the glass appear to fill the whole space. The materials were kept simple as well as the office layout making it a light and efficient building. The building was intended to be bare concrete but was painted a neutral beige colour.

One of the distinctive features of the building was the auditorium at the east end, which protrudes out the end of the building and is decorated with long vertical notches. The thinking at the time was that auditoriums needed to be horn shaped. Hollingsworth disagreed with this assumption but was over ruled by the client. The building has since been demolished.

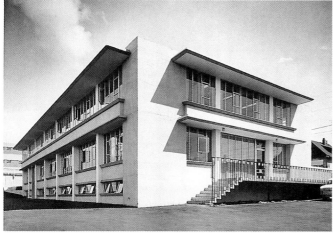

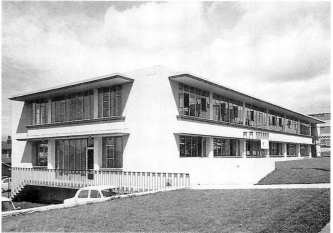

# S h a n d r o  1950/51

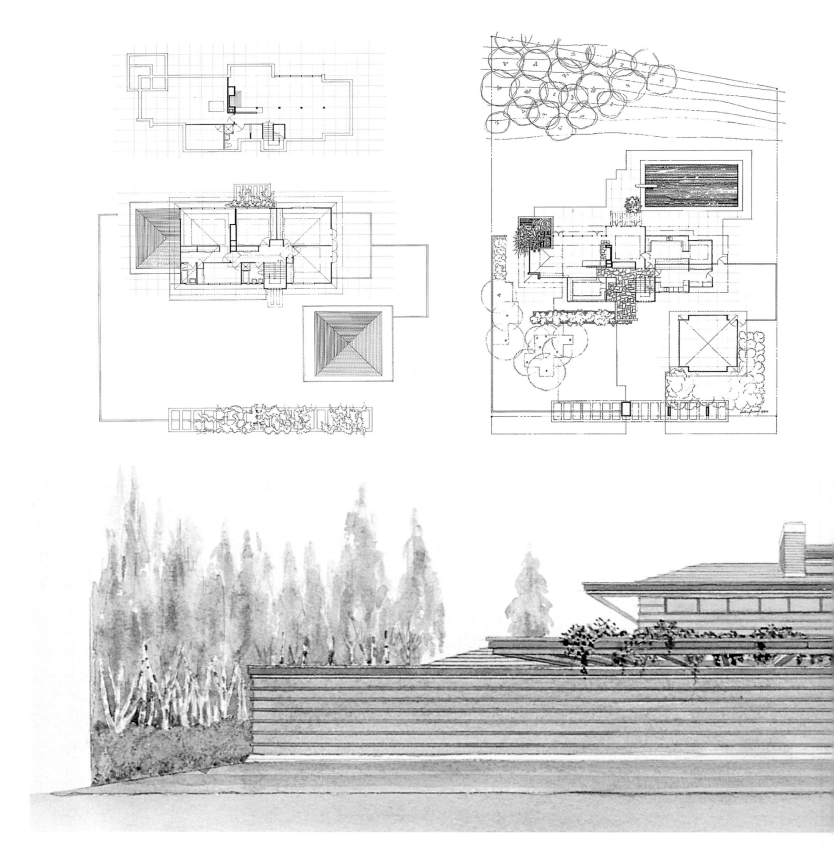

This large house is located on a west facing river front site in Edmonton. The overall look of the house is reminiscent of Frank Lloyd Wright's prairie houses with its simple pitched roofs with large overhangs. The house was constructed of cedar board and batten inside and out with the wood stained not painted.

The living room is at the back facing the river and has a large 40-foot long window wall. All the ceilings are open to the roof with light shelves that provide indirect lighting. There is also a large patio at the back and a pool. The building is still extant today in its original form.

# Dalby 1958

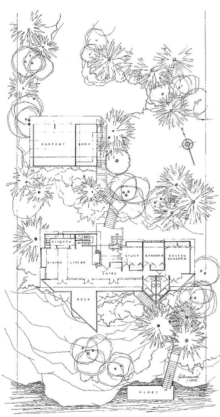

Built on a steep, rocky, well-treed site that slopes to the sea, the house appears to float over the landscape. A large cantilevered porch provides outdoor living and creates a feeling of freedom and suspension for its occupants. The roof forms are kept simple and slope in sympathy with the site, providing a strong sheltering feeling within.

All materials are natural and relate to the site. The chimney stone are rocks from the site. Cedar was used inside and out. The roof structure is beam joists at two-foot centre and left exposed. Concrete is exposed aggregate for interior and exterior finishes.

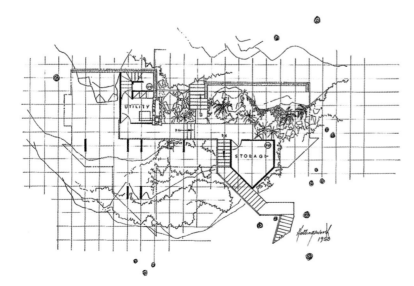

# Showhouse 1959/60

Designed as a show
house for developer
Eric Allen for one of his
projects in the Fraser
Valley, but never built.
The design is a precursor
to the Trethewey house
and has many similarities,
such as concrete block
and cedar construction
and even a circular pool.
The idea of a curve came
from the passage of the
sun during the day.
Maximum light can be
achieved if the house is
oriented on an east/west
axis. A curved structure
also gives a series of
limited vistas through
the spaces and sets up
a different relationship
moving through those
spaces.

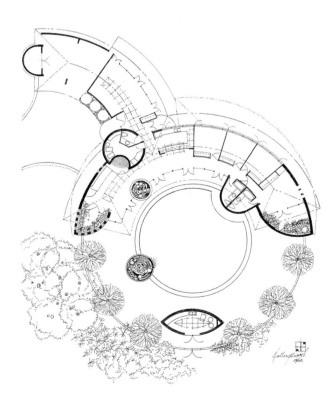

# Trethewey I 1959

The house is situated in a small meadow, which had several large cedar trees, and a bowl shaped hillock rising to the windward side and facing towards the southwest. The house is nestled into the rise to fit the circular bowl. The house curves around and opens onto a circular pool.

The building is on a heated radiant slab with a rear wall of concrete and masonry set against the side of the hill. The walls are milled cedar board partitions, both inside and out and the floor finish throughout is terrazzo. The bedrooms have private gardens. In the living area, a small garden pool flows indoor and outdoor, separated by the glass walls. Ceilings are all cedar boards patterned to the roof form, and all rooms are illuminated by indirect lighting from light shelves on all sides of each room.

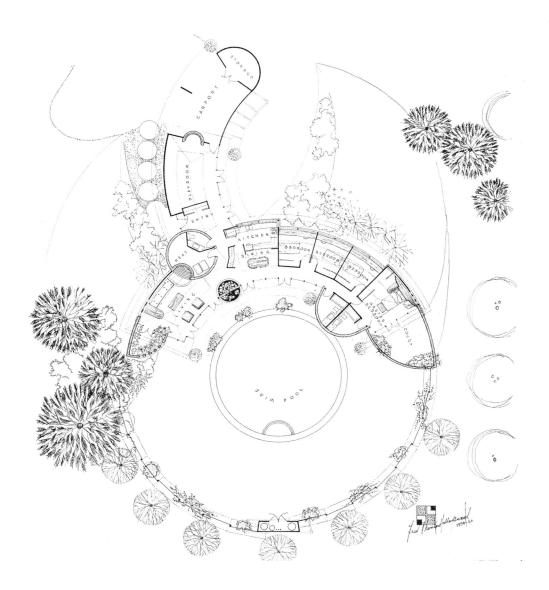

# Pullan Studio 1960

This small photographic studio and darkroom is situated next to a fine old shingled residence. The studio is linked by a covered walkway to the existing house. The materials for the studio and the roof match those of the main house. The studio is set into the slope of the lot and provides two levels with the upper for the darkroom and a large open studio below.

The building has simple frame walls finished on the exterior with cedar shingles, while the interior is white painted drywall. The south and west walls are floor to ceiling windows. A small reflecting pool was placed beside the stairwell constructed of exposed concrete, as were the floor, steps and terrace.

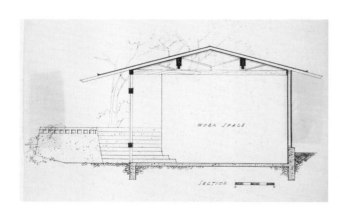

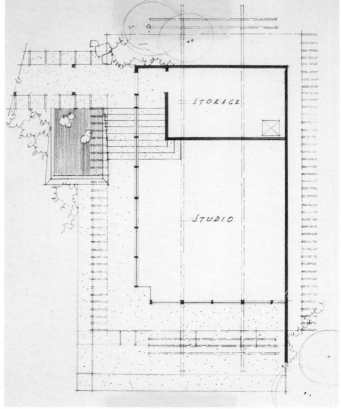

# Banks 1961

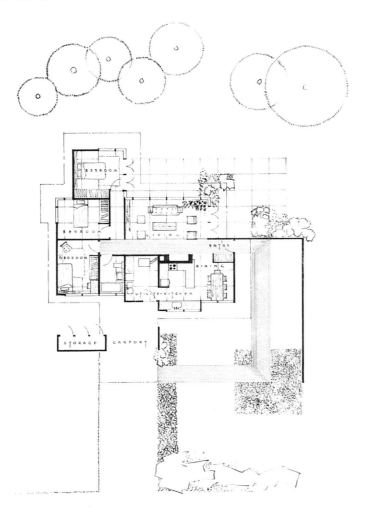

This simple wood house sits on a large lot and is oriented to the garden at the rear. It has an open plan with the fireplace separating the dining room from the kitchen and the living room. The building is constructed on a slab with radiant warm air heating. Cedar channel siding was used on both the inside and outside. It has a flat roof with clerestory windows and ceiling coves that provide indirect lighting at a cosy sense of scale.

The windows were designed to be as economical as possible, utilizing wooden mullions in proportions designed to be attractive and the corners allowing for an expression of openness and visual freedom.

RESIDENCE FOR MR & MRS REG BANKS
Fred Hollingsworth Arch. Designer.

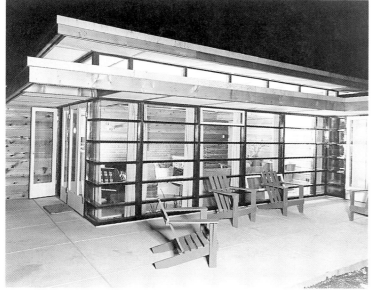

Middle Work 1960-1979

# McGrath House and Pavilion 1960 and 1969

The house was situated on a large lakefront lot that was landscaped by previous owners. The house was designed so that no trees were cut or moved and as a result a flowering cherry is allowed to come through the upper porch floor. The house was located at the bottom of a gentle slope before the site flattens to the lakeshore. Built with three floor levels; the entry and children's rooms, the upper living and kitchen and master bedroom, and the lower playroom, guestroom, study and service rooms.

The walls are finished both inside and out in twelve-inch clear redwood boards with mahogany battens. The ceilings and exterior soffits are white sand plaster throughout. The entry, corridor and bath are exposed concrete, as well as the hearth and lintels of the fireplace and the pool at the entry. Skylights open the room to natural light and are used as a night lighting source, along with concealed lighting from flat soffits.

All the furniture was designed and detailed by the architect and custom made on the job with fabrics and carpets selected to complete the interior colour and texture balance. The entry pool flows inside and out and acts as a reminder of the lake beyond.

The pavilion was designed as a guest cottage with the main space featuring a fifteen-foot diameter skylight of coloured plastic. The room has a large fireplace of red brick and views to the lake. It has a kitchen, bathroom and a small bedroom. Care was taken in the siting of the pavilion in relation to the main house, the landscaping and its close relationship to the lakefront and beach.

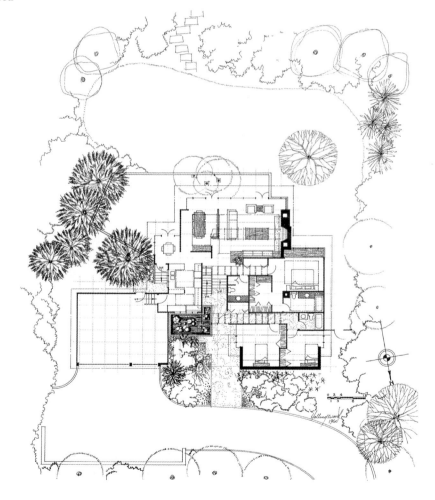

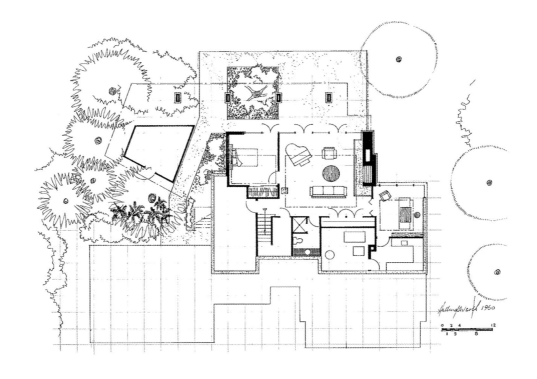

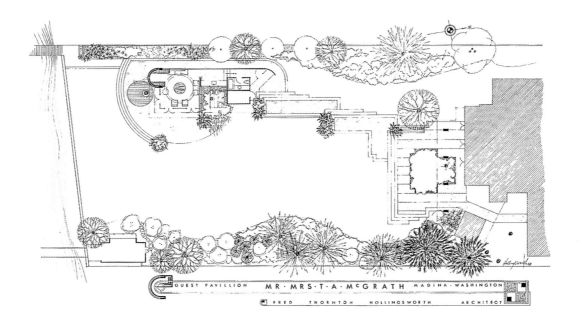

GUEST PAVILLION    MR·MRS·T·A·McGRATH    MADINA·WASHINGTON

FRED THORNTON HOLLINGSWORTH    ARCHITECT

# Berkeley Hospital 1960/61

Considered at the time an innovative approach to hospital design, the building is constructed as a cross form, that provides corridor surveillance from the single nurse's station. Each wing is designed for varying wards, public, private and semi-private, with lounges and utility rooms for each wing. The fourth wing is for services and offices. The entry core is at the centre and features a tall light filled atrium space.

The floor is terrazzo on slab and the exterior walls are concrete and glass. The walls and partitions and roof are wood frame, finished in cedar board and batten. The interior and exterior walls are of the same materials. The intent was to create a warm home-like atmosphere, to avoid an institutional feeling and to help, by way of the environment to support rehabilitation.

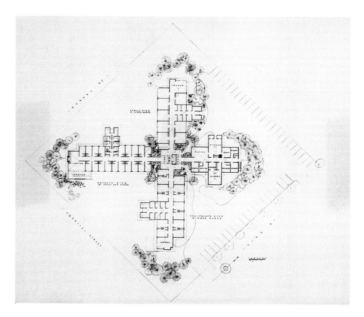

# Lees 1961

Designed as a completely circular house constructed on a slab with wood and a concrete block wall at the back and sited into a hillside. The house was a two-story structure with living spaces on the main floor and bedrooms radiating around the upper floor. The stairs went around the core. The carport was also a circular structure. The Lees house is an example of the organic principles applied to issues of economics. It was economic to use new forms and shapes, and the results are often much more interesting than the square box. Unfortunately, the house was never built.

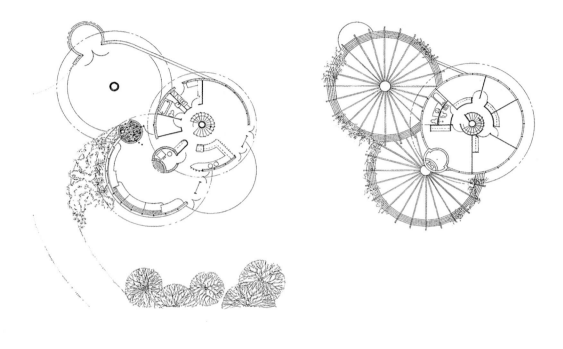

# Maltby 1962

The house sits on a flat shelf of a sloping lot with impressive views. Its semi-circular form takes advantage of the dramatic site. The client requested the house have an oriental feel and the influence of Japanese architecture can be seen in the design of the detail that holds the eaves on the roof and the various proportions of the windows and interior spaces. The exterior and interior finishes are stucco and plaster with dark stained battens. One of the main features is a large deck that sweeps around the front of the house and large windows that provide access to the deck from the interior. The house was awarded a Massey Medal in 1962.

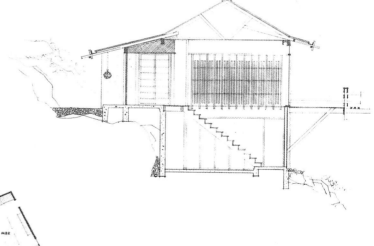

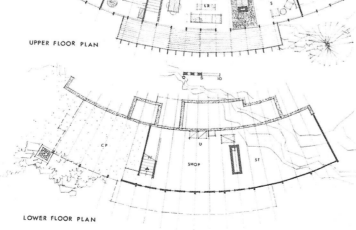

UPPER FLOOR PLAN

LOWER FLOOR PLAN

# Frackson 1963

The plan of the house centres on an enclosed atrium with a pool, fountain and plantings located between the living room and the office/study. All the major rooms open on to the terrace and garden at the rear of the house. The garden also extends into the living area in the form of large elevated planting beds. The house is finished in white stucco and stained cedar inside and out. The interior spaces have a low soffit at seven feet with the ceilings then extending up to ten feet. All the floors are terrazzo of white marble. The house has a flat roof with the upper wall slightly angled inward giving an increased sense of relation to the ground. The furniture was designed by the architect and built by the client.

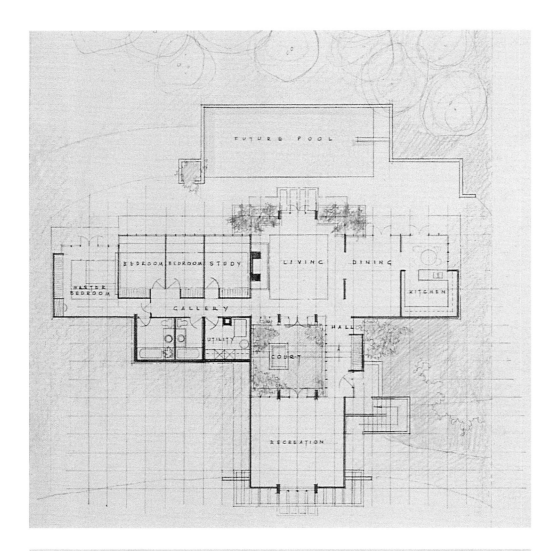

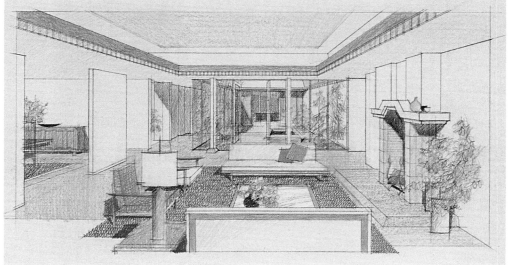

# Van Winckle 1968

The house is raised on a podium to obscure any vision into the house from the street. The design centres on an interior court to create a quiet, private space that the living room and pool conservatory open onto. The scale of the building is intimate, and its relation to the rear of site locks it to the landscaped natural surroundings. The roof forms are intended to relate to the hills and valleys of the setting. The interior spaces have large soffits and the ceilings have skylights with decorative patterning. Both the exterior and interior are finished in natural cedar boards. The ceilings and soffits are plaster and the floors are terrazzo.

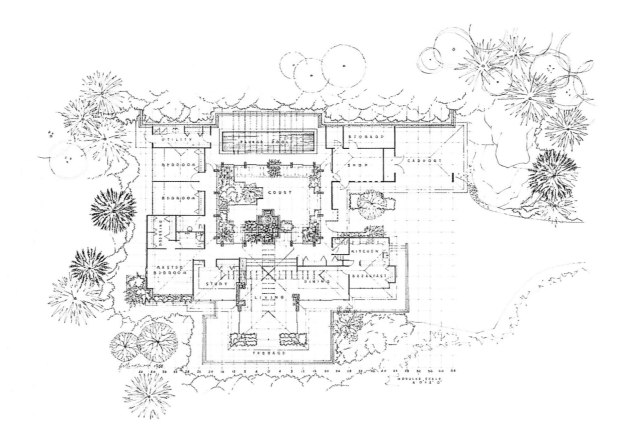

# Hoffer 1971

Located on a rocky lot, the house is set on a deep podium retaining wall to the south, sand filled and slab construction for the house and terraces. The floors are on two levels, one for the dining room and down for the living room. The living room, dining and kitchen are at 45-degrees and covered by a high tent-like roof with a skylight at the peak. A massive granite fireplace stack penetrates the living and dining room. Granite from the site blasting was used for the fireplace.

All rooms face the view except the kitchen, which looks to the mountains to the northeast. The 45-degree plan is used throughout and all the ceilings are open to the pitch. Doors open from all rooms to the terraces. The house turns away from the street and nestles behind a rock mound that rises some eight feet above the street level. All the walls are cedar boards and the masonry walls are granite from the site. The ceilings are also cedar boards and the floors are terrazzo and carpet.

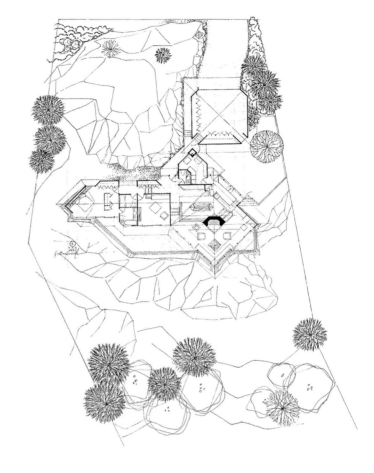

# Rudden 1971

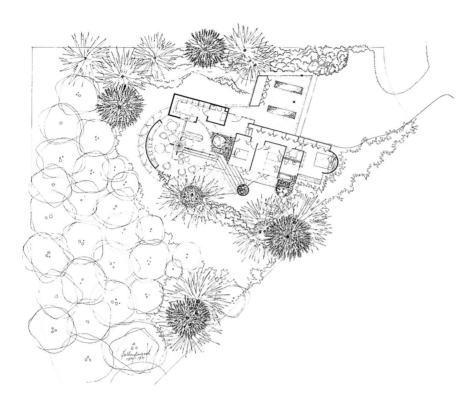

The clients already owned a beautiful site upon which they decided to build. The large lot had a steep slope to the view side of Burrard Inlet and Vancouver Island. The plan was designed to make the view visible from all the bedrooms, entry, living room and dining area in a linear form. The plan consists of a complete circular area containing the living and dining spaces. A solid rectangle of stepped concrete block encloses the work area of the kitchen and utility rooms, which are skylit.

The entry, which joins the living areas to the bedroom wing, creates the opportunity for a garden planting space between the two areas. The bedrooms are contained within a linear from with a passage/storage hall and two bedrooms. The master bedroom completes the wing with its two baths. The master bath has its own obscure white plastic screen wall for privacy with an intimate garden and pool along side the bath.

The construction was simple frame walls (except the kitchen cube) finished inside and out in white sandfloat stucco plaster with trim boards. The ceilings are exposed fir beams and cedar boards with natural finish in all rooms. The fireplace at the living space centre is of welded steel sheet and approximately six feet in diameter with a base firebox of concrete block. A cone and smoke pipe of steel is supported on four poured concrete fins, which also support the roof beams. Overhead, around the smokestack are six clear plastic standard circular skylights for light and sun. The fireplace steel is painted black. All rooms as shown have direct access to the terraces and garden. The double carport and storage closets are the same construction as elsewhere. Apart from the driveway, terraces and built areas, all the natural growth and trees were retained in natural form.

# UBC Faculty of Law 1971

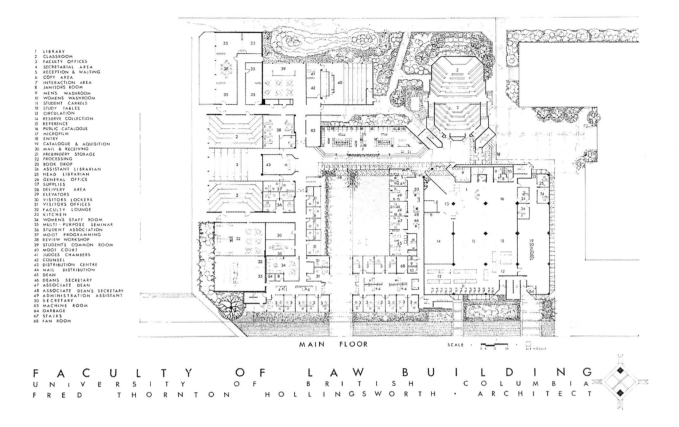

1  LIBRARY
2  CLASSROOM
3  FACULTY OFFICES
4  SECRETARIAL AREA
5  RECEPTION & WAITING
6  COPY AREA
7  INTERACTION AREA
8  JANITORS ROOM
9  MEN'S WASHROOM
10  WOMEN'S WASHROOM
11  STUDENT CARRELS
12  STUDY TABLES
13  CIRCULATION
14  RESERVE COLLECTION
15  REFERENCE
16  PUBLIC CATALOGUE
17  MICROFILM
18  ENTRY
19  CATALOGUE & AQUISITION
20  MAIL & RECEIVING
21  PREBINDERY STORAGE
22  PROCESSING
23  BOOK DROP
24  ASSISTANT LIBRARIAN
25  HEAD LIBRARIAN
26  GENERAL OFFICE
27  SUPPLIES
28  DELIVERY AREA
29  ELEVATORS
30  VISITORS LOCKERS
31  VISITORS OFFICES
32  FACULTY LOUNGE
33  KITCHEN
34  WOMEN'S STAFF ROOM
35  MULTI-PURPOSE SEMINAR
36  STUDENT ASSOCIATION
37  MOOT PROGRAMMING
38  REVIEW WORKSHOP
39  STUDENTS COMMON ROOM
40  MOOT COURT
41  JUDGES CHAMBERS
42  COUNSEL
43  DISTRIBUTION CENTRE
44  MAIL DISTRIBUTION
45  DEAN
46  DEANS SECRETARY
47  ASSOCIATE DEAN
48  ASSOCIATE DEAN'S SECRETARY
49  ADMINISTRATION ASSISTANT
50  SECRETARY
63  MACHINE ROOM
64  GARBAGE
67  STAIRS
68  FAN ROOM

MAIN FLOOR       SCALE ·

FACULTY OF LAW BUILDING
UNIVERSITY OF BRITISH COLUMBIA
FRED THORNTON HOLLINGSWORTH · ARCHITECT

The building houses the law library, classrooms, auditorium and faculty offices. The all-concrete structure is integrated with an existing building. There is a generous inner courtyard with lots of seating and a large common area on the inside. The students appreciate the fact that the faculty must walk through the common area to get to their offices. This allows for an opportunity for access to the faculty by students.

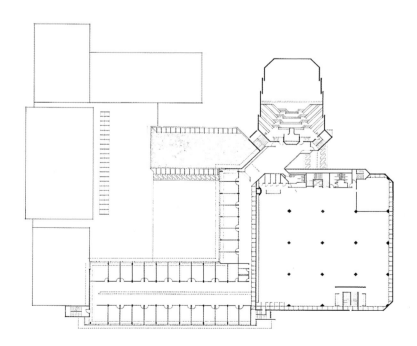

COURT ENTRANCE

# Straight 1972

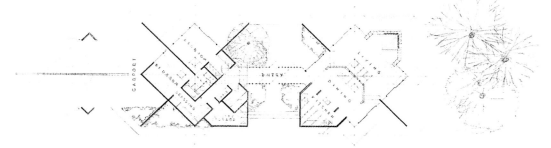

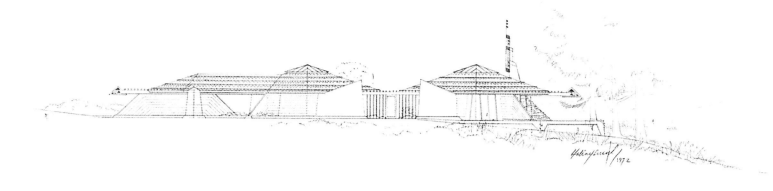

The concept was very simple and clean, consisting of two square pavilions each twenty-four feet square with an added projection on the landside for services. These two pavilions are spaced apart by a common terrace on the waterfront side and an entry terrace on the landside. The entrance corridor connects them and is covered by an inside-outside trellis. This continuous trellis is roofed with clear glass where required. It also continues through the house, living room, bedrooms, carport and out into the landscape.

From the entry to the right are the kitchen, dining and down three small steps the living room. A large stone fireplace is the only solid exterior wall. All other exterior surface walls in this room are floor to ceiling glazing, all rooms exit to the terraces. A low rail wall of cedar boards separates the living from the dining areas. Cabinets separate the kitchen from the dining space. From the entry on the left are two bedrooms, bath and utility room. The floors are concrete slab with radiant heating. Ceilings are cedar boards to the roof pattern.

All interior and exterior walls are finished in the same cedar boards, except the utility and kitchen projections, which are stucco (sandfloat) in a pale beige colour. Roofs are of cedar shingles with skylights of aluminum extrusions and solar double glazed units top both square room blocks. Terraces are concrete slabs on sidewall footings with edge walls. Patterning is various combinations of exposed aggregate inserts, strip inserts and smooth cast panels. A double carport is provided. Landscape beds are kept simple with natural local species of shrubs, flowers and trees.

# Stewart 1973

The house was built in Utah next to a large park on a steep lot with dramatic views. Constructed of concrete with wood roofs the house has five bedrooms, each with its own garden space. It has a large terrace to the view and the living room opens out onto the terrace. The angled roofline relates to the slope of the site. There are separate roofs for each of the spaces of the house.

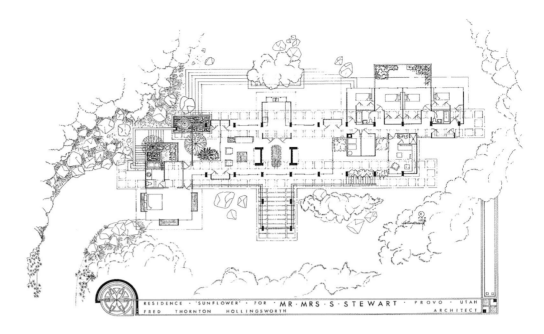

RESIDENCE · 'SUNFLOWER' · FOR · MR · MRS · S · STEWART · PROVO · UTAH
FRED THORNTON HOLLINGSWORTH ARCHITECT

# Ducommun 1975

This residence was designed for Mr. and Mrs. Kenneth Ducommon in 1975, and was intended to be built on the outskirts of Brussels. The client, an industrial design engineer with his own practice, wanted a modern house similar to what was being built at the time in his native Canada. The design was carried out to meet his specific needs, which included residential spaces plus a work office mezzanine over the living room. Also, a garage and workshop for his collection of five antique cars. The residence was to be clay brick walls with B.C. cedar siding, both inside and out. Floors were to be radiant heated concrete slabs, coloured and polished.

The exterior two-story windows were screened for heat control by decorative cedar strips with coloured space brackets. Access from all main floor rooms to the garden was provided and an exterior cantilevered porch was included for the second floor bedrooms. The main entry space with indoor-outdoor garden pool was used to separate the residence and the garage workshop.

The mansard roof form was used to conform to the code for roof slopes and the brick was also a stated code requirement. The roof (mansard) slopes were finished in cedar. The hidden flat roof within the facia form was not permitted to be visible. All interior and exterior walls were brick or cedar surfaces. All brick vertical joints were flush mortar, all horizontal joints were raked out, and garage doors were the same cedar boards.

Unfortunately the owner made a decision to return to Canada and the house was not built.

# Moon II  1979

Built on a large acreage near Calgary, the plan revolves around a garden court. The interior is a generous open plan, with all the widows facing south. Brick is used extensively in the house for the chimney stacks and all the floors are brick. The roof is made up of three parts each one tucked into the other, that echo the prairie ground plane. The garage/workshop has a large triangular skylight.

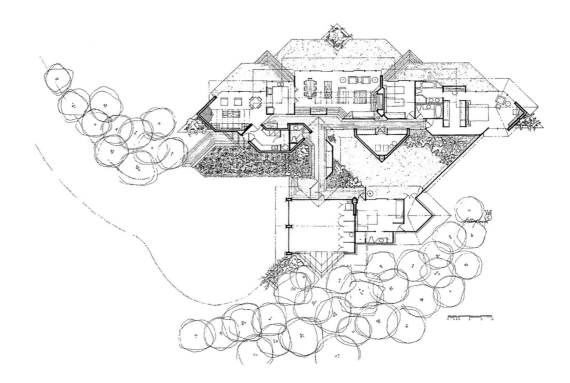

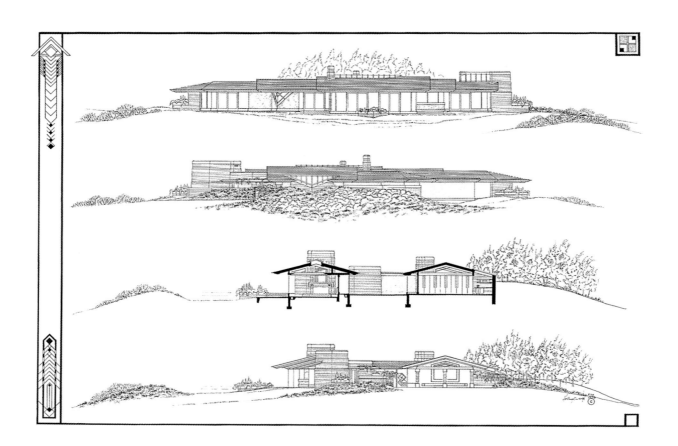

Later Work 1980-1994

# Fluckiger 1982

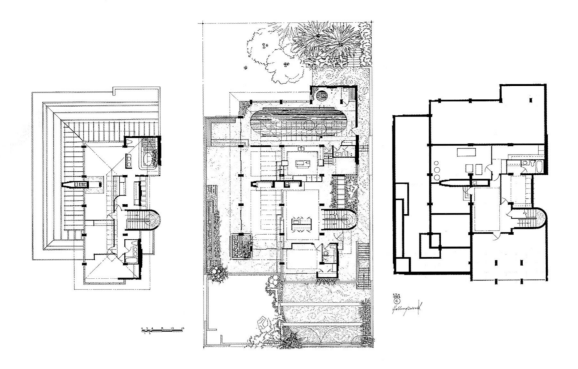

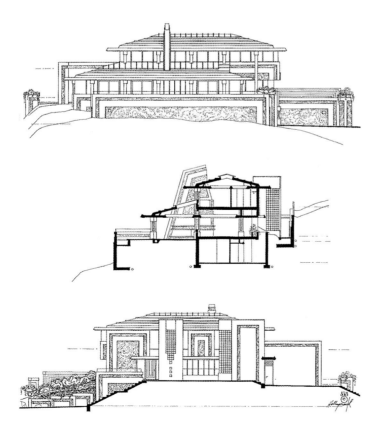

Built on a sloping lot with beautiful views of the bay to the west, the house is three stories and constructed of poured concrete. The living room has a large deck that takes advantage of the view; it also has an interior garden. There is a covered pool at the back and extensive gardens; the roof is made of copper.

# Malmgren 1986

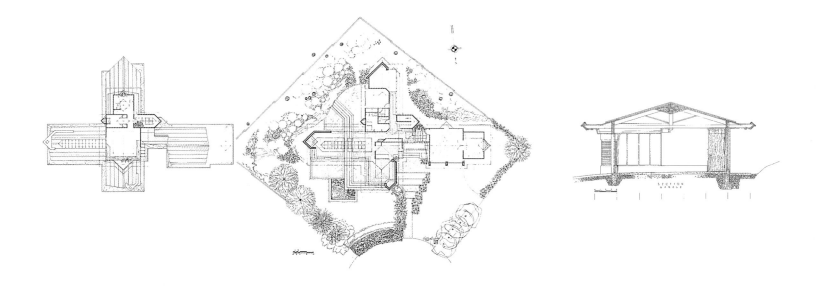

The house features a living room with glass on both sides and a fireplace at one end. The garden terrace runs from the back through to the front of the house. There are two bedrooms down and stairs that lead up to the master bedroom. Both the exterior and interior is finished with cedar board and batten. The ceilings have large soffits with indirect lighting and then open above. The house displays many similarities to houses of Frank Lloyd Wright, yet retains a distinctive West Coast feel.

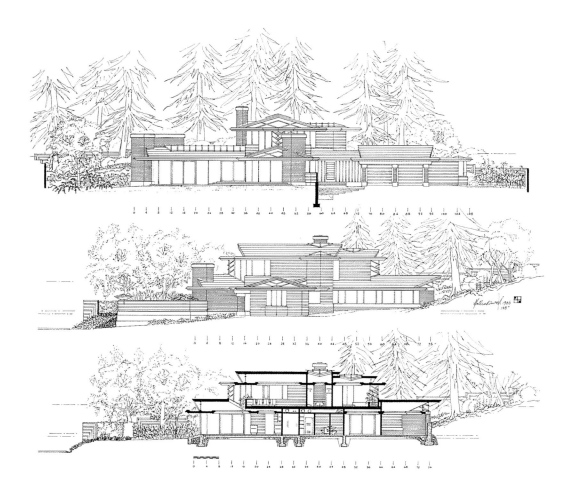

# Trethewey II 1987

This second residence for Mr. and Mrs. Richard Trethewey is built on a large property in the country and features a man-made lake. The house has three bedrooms, with the living room, dining room and kitchen in one block that looks out towards the lake. The bedrooms also view the lake and are in another block, connected by a glazed entry area. The garage and workshop are in a third block. All three blocks are ingeniously connected by a glazed covered trellis, which carries vines and provides a strong horizontal feeling. The walls are square except for the corners, which are slightly angled inward and give the house a connection to the ground. Stucco was used both for the exterior and interior and the ceilings are open to the roof. The whole result is a luxurious comfortable residence for rural living.

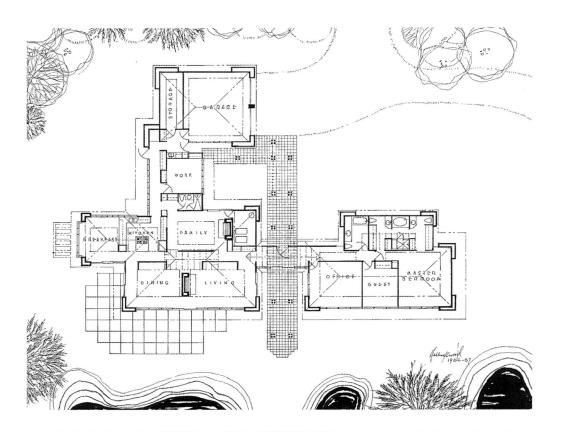

# Plommer 1989

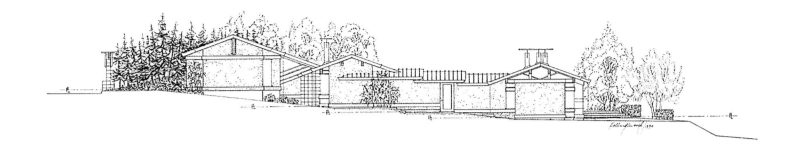

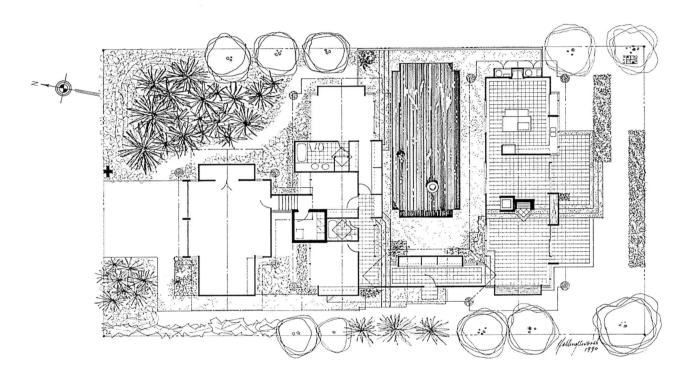

The residence was built in Kamloops B.C. on the golf course, riverside. The house centres on a private court with a swimming pool. The living room looks into the pool area as does the bedrooms. The lot has a slight slope and several roofs were used that follow down the slope. Wood frame construction was used with stucco and concrete block walls inside and out. The fireplace is masonry for the fireplace firebox with metal exposed flues to the roof above. Metal was also used for the roofs, which are wood frame with open interior ceilings of exposed fir beams and cedar planks.

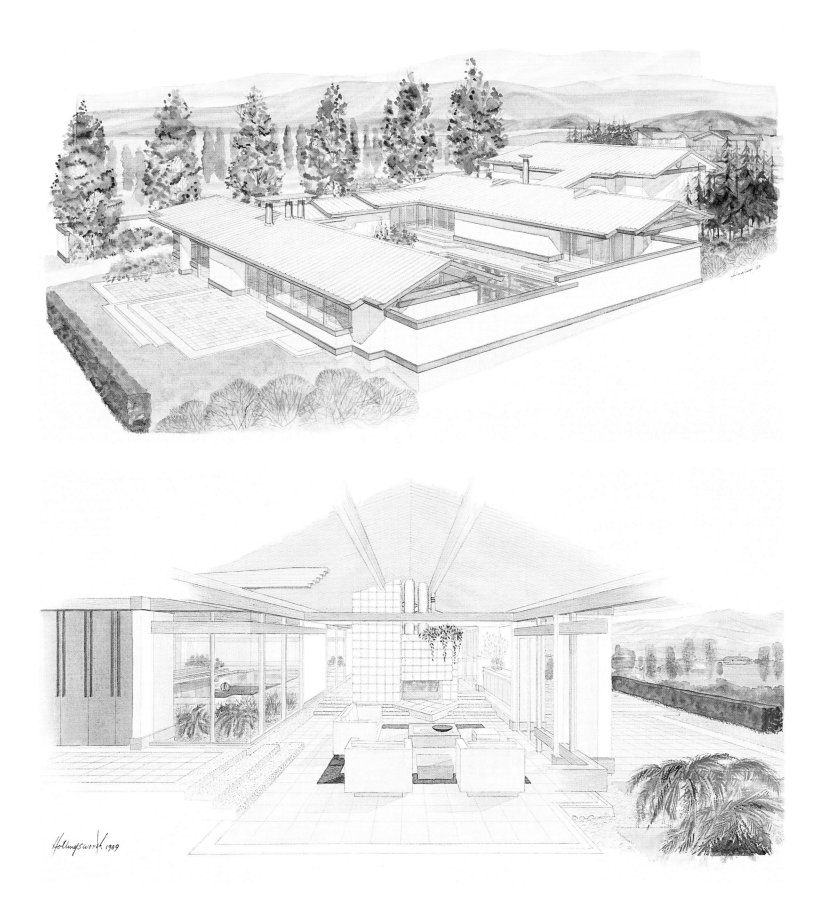

# Smith 1990

Built on a triangular lot
in West Vancouver with
a commanding view of
the city, the house sits
in a walled enclosure to
provide maximum privacy.
The multi-levels of the
house take full advantage
of the view afforded by the
sloping lot. The house
features an elevator from
the garage off the lane,
and a pool next to the
kitchen and nook. The
design incorporates
curved rooms at two
ends, one the kitchen
nook and the other
the home office. The
construction materials are
wood frame with stucco
both inside and out.

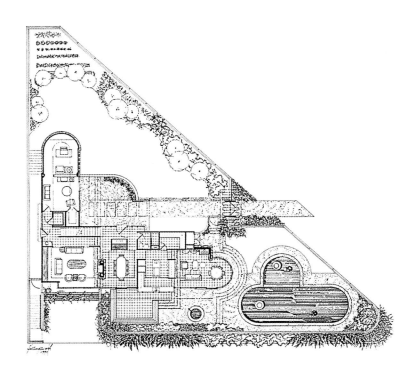

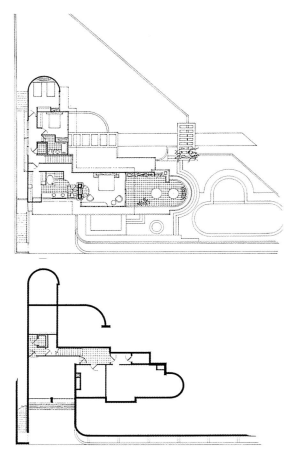

# Bosa 1990

Built on three lots with a wonderful water view, the house is made up of several curves and circular forms that follow the contours down the site. The curved and circular spaces create a sense of freed space and form and provide a great visual diversity for the eye. Decorative elements are incorporated throughout the house and gardens, from the etched glass doors of the entry, to the concrete work and garden planters. Every element of the house expresses the interrelatedness of the design. The large multi-level house features a two-story circular living room with floor to ceiling windows, an indoor pool with a skylight and all the rooms of the house have access to the outside. Concrete was used extensively in the construction along with stucco. The roofs are made of beautifully shaped copper panels that have been allowed to weather. The large enclosed swimming pool, sauna bath and hot tub are in a space with a separate sitting area and fireplace with an access to the terrace. The ocean is visible while swimming.

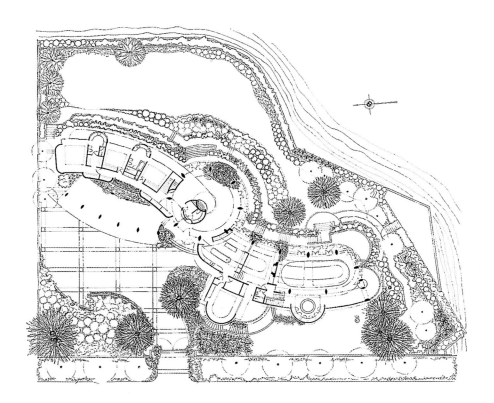

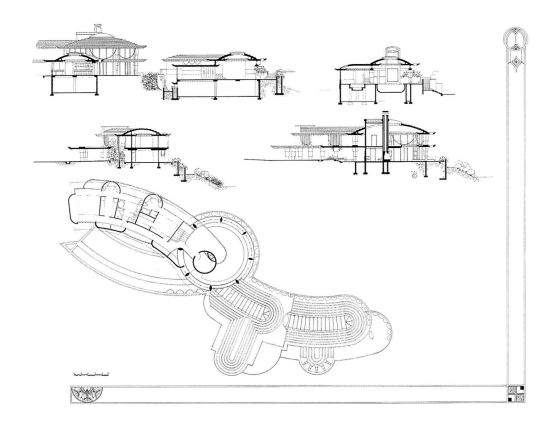

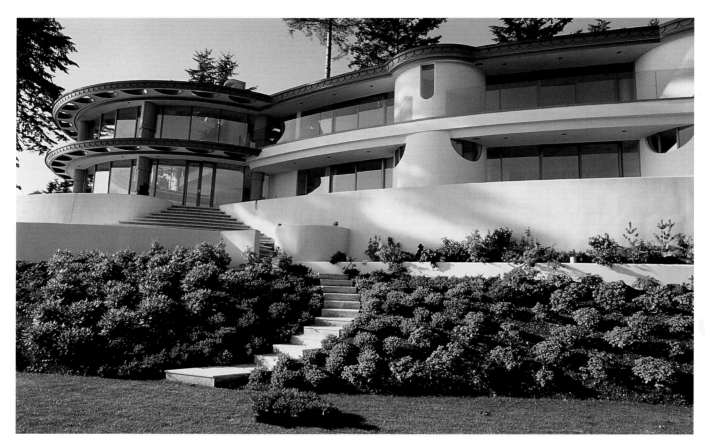

# Kassam 1994

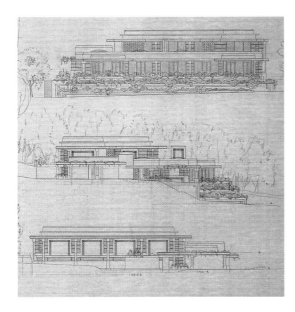

The client requested that the house have a warm and friendly feeling and an Islamic flavour. This is reflected in the geometric pattern in the concrete walls of the courtyard and its reflecting pool. The house is designed round the courtyard with rooms entering into the court. There is access from the courtyard that goes right through the house providing a great sense of openness and integration of inside and outside. Glass walls are used to capitalize on the views and open onto a large terrace. The second story contains the bedrooms, with living spaces and a master bedroom on the main floor. There are three large circular skylights in the dining room, kitchen and the entry spaces. The living room has five concrete columns, with glazing and exit doors between to access the view to the city, inlet and the terrace on the north. Access and glazing to the court area is provided on the south side.

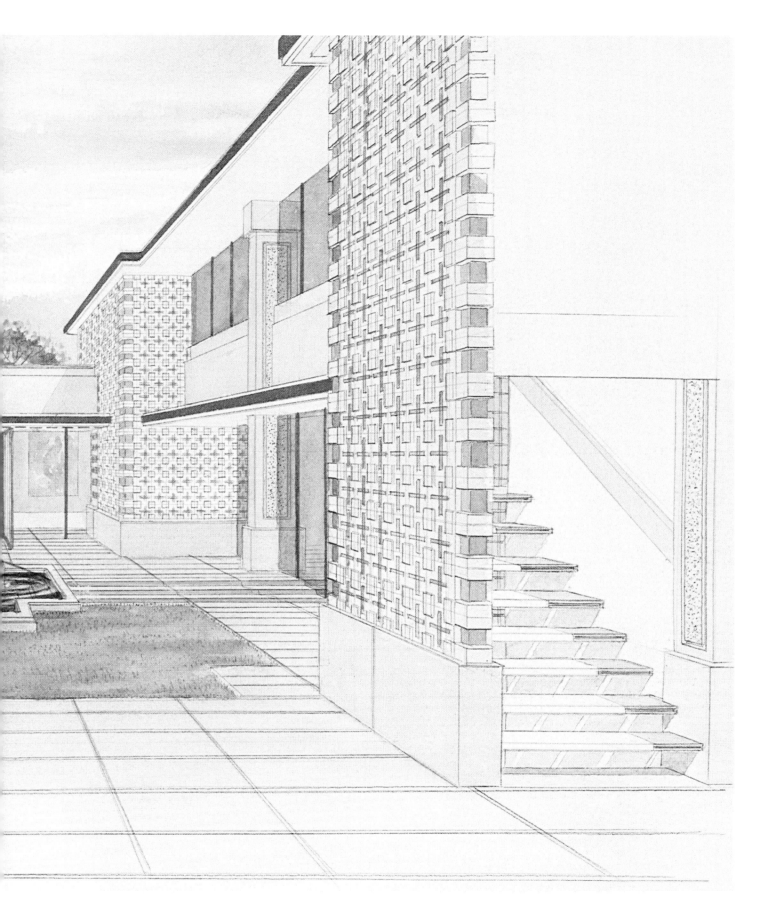

# Villa Environmatic

The "Enviromatic House" is an attempt to create a building that is "friendly" to the environment. This design does not use any oils for its heating process and attempts by today's technology to least disturb the environment. It is intended to create a new experience in spatial living and a more natural environment for its occupants.

The various living spaces and entrance are oriented around the central solar collector atrium, which serves as a spacious, indoor landscape and collects the solar heated volumes. At the top of this area is a large duct which, in the summer season, exhausts the solar heat to the exterior at each end. In the cooler seasons these exhausts are closed automatically and the collected solar heat is circulated to the lower floor outlets and used to heat the building. In addition, an automatically controlled heat pump is used to augment any additional heating required to the solar source.

During summer, outdoor cool air is used to replace the solar air, which has been exhausted. Solar heat panels provide domestic hot water and electrical sources augment any additional hot water requirements for dull days. Large glazed areas are used in between the collector atrium and the living spaces.

Construction is of decorated concrete blocks, square in size and insulated within. Glu-lam or metal arches are intended over the collector space with a double glazed closure. Other roofing is standard frame with plaster ceilings and insulation within. Floors are concrete slab and appropriate tile or stone finishes as desired. Walls, other than the block, are standard frame and plaster-stucco, sandfloat finish.

All sewage disposal waters will be via a heat-exchanged system to relieve the heat volumes from the disposals and return them to the system for reuse, for example, in domestic hot water. Solar radiant floor heating systems for warm water are also under consideration as a moderate comfort addition to reduce further the need for any combustible fuel system. It is obvious the "Environmatic House" is within reach and its various methods and systems will become common as further interest develops for our living environment.

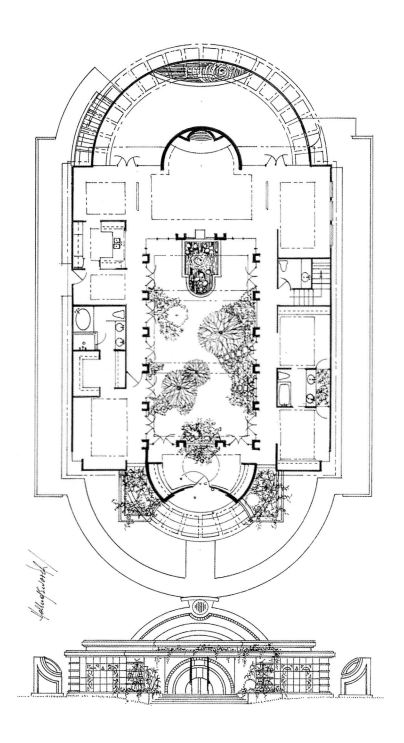

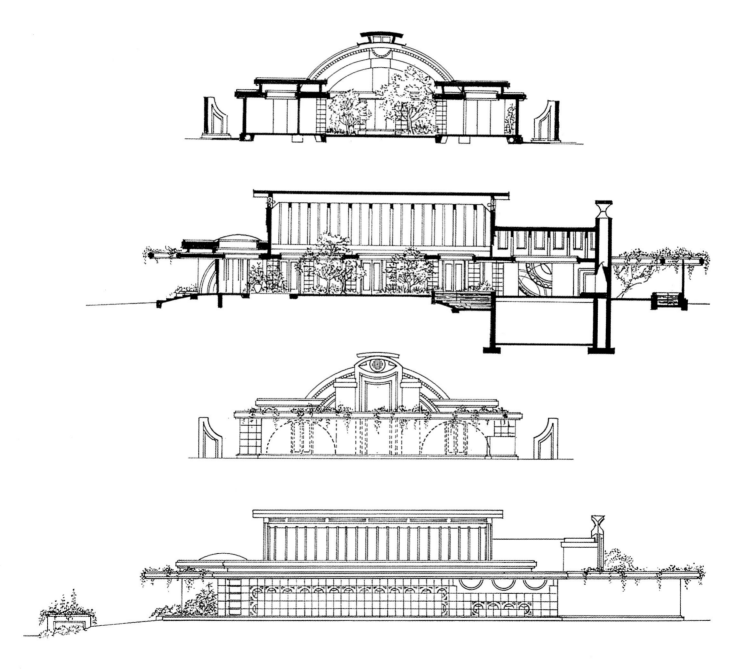

# Villa Tri-Partite I

The "Tri-Partite" house was designed with the intent of creating a new kind of environmental living space, within the present and future city environment. The principle design idea was to enclose a private garden within the building limits of a lot size site, creating an environment of quiet and privacy not commonly seen in the design of current residences.

Based on a triangular module (equilateral triangles), the room spaces (except perhaps the kitchen and entry areas), are all designed to look inwards toward the enclosed wall garden areas. Thus creating a quiet controlled environment that can be totally private and undisturbed to a great extent by the outside city.

The plan consists of three triangular pavilions (or "living cells") connected by linked glazed passages. These cells and passages are all glazed to the garden and all open onto it for seasonal access and ventilation.

The three "cells" serve various residential purposes (1) for reception, living and working, (2) for sleeping and dressing, (3) for play or recreation and utility functions. The roofs are pitched triangles with inset upper glazing hips.

The cell ceilings follow the roof forms for the interiors and the corridors also have pitched roofs. All floors are radiant heated coloured concrete slabs.

The garden itself is in three area sections for various light, sun and shade conditions. The garden is separated by a large water garden, with fountains or moving water features. A partial swim pool could also be devised as part of this space if desired.

The whole arrangement and planning is to create a quiet, peaceful, interrelated functioning space, which offers many varying spaces for comfort, privacy and quiet both inside and outside. A private intimate space in which to escape from the busy pace of the city environment.

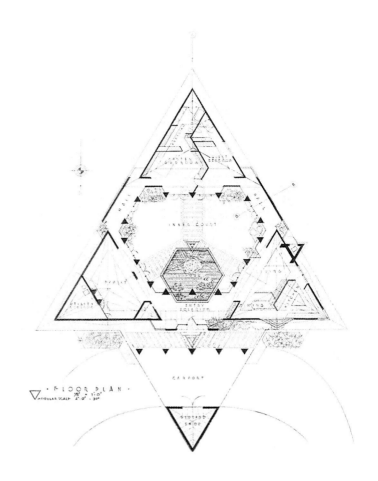

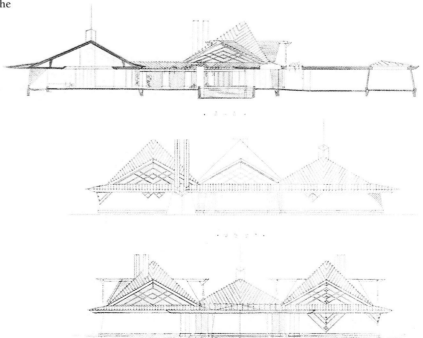

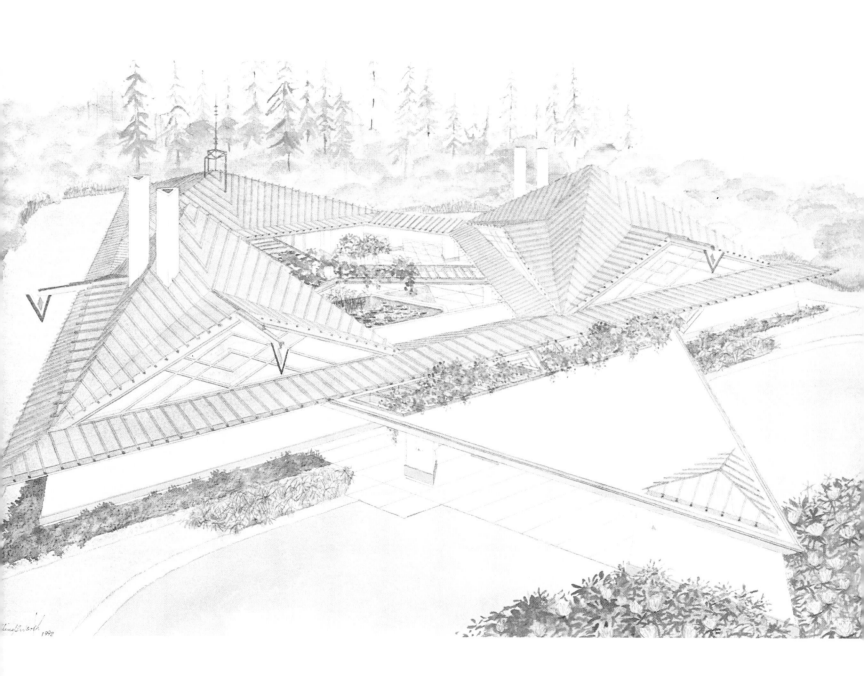

# Villa Tri-Partite II

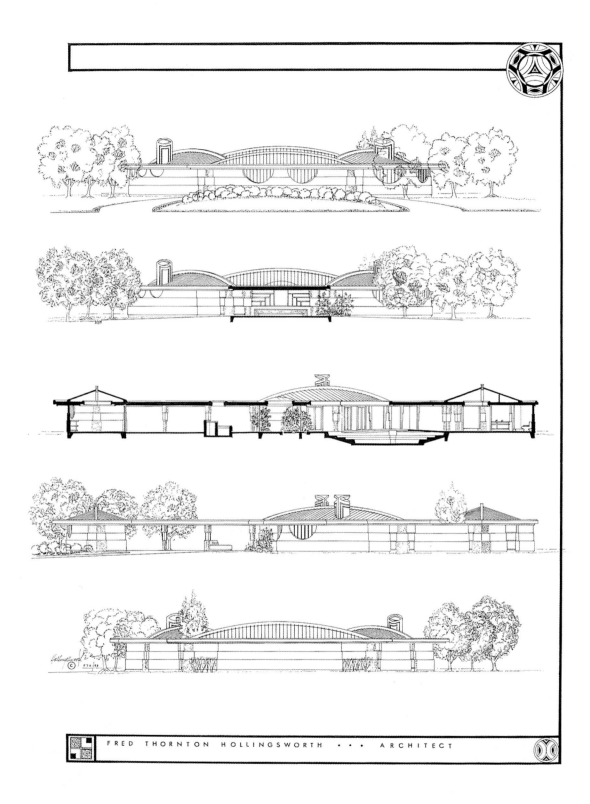

FRED THORNTON HOLLINGSWORTH • • • ARCHITECT

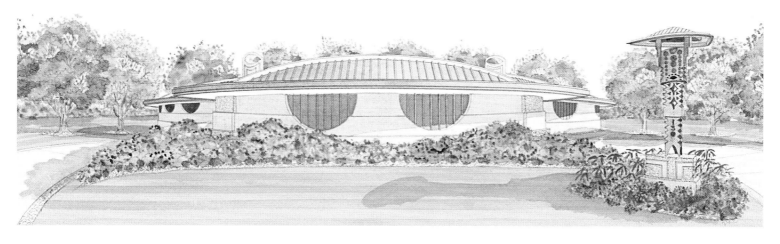

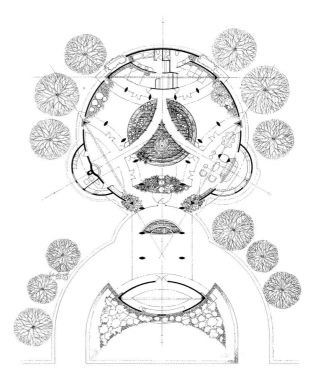

Designed on the same principles of organic architecture as the triangular "Tri-Partite" house and intended to follow the same functions and environmental ideals, it is based rather on a circular modular form. It illustrates the idea that buildings designed with a similar function need not in any way resemble each other's forms or esthetics. It is another example of the "turned inside" planning that can provide an escape from external city patterns, and allow a peaceful, quiet, and private environment.

The plan varies in some ways from the triangular tri-partite plan. The three "living cells" are linked by bridges, which create a walkway over the garden pool and meet at a central quiet "sitting" area. The three "living cells" contain the functions shown, and are similar to the triangular plan. However, many various arrangements of function and space are possible for specific uses and desires. The cells in this design are roofed with copper on wood decking. Both of these tri-partite designs are intended to show concern for the natural environment as described in the "environmental house" and, to the greatest extent possible, utilize current technology to protect it.

# Acknowledgements

WE WOULD LIKE TO TAKE THIS OPPORTUNITY TO EXPRESS OUR APPRECIATION TO THOSE INDIVIDUALS WHO contributed to the realization of this publication. Firstly, our thanks must go to Fred Hollingsworth and his wife Phyllis for providing access to their archives and for the many hours they spent locating and generating material. Without their generosity and hospitality, the project could not have been realized. Our thanks also to those who contributed to the publication in particular Rhodri Windsor Liscombe whose essay provides an articulate analysis of Fred Hollingsworth's work in the context of both regional and international architectural practices. The forward by Barry Downs, long time friend and former partner provides a personal perspective that is greatly appreciated. An essential aspect of this book is the photography by Selwyn Pullan, which so accurately and sensitively illustrate Hollingsworth's houses. The design of the book by Elisa Gutiérrez has resulted in a publication that is elegant and thoughtfully constructed. We also extend our thanks to the following for their help and support in this project: Russell Hollingsworth, Cedric Bomford, Miguel da Conceicao, Mike Banwell and Sherry McKay.

The research and material in this publication was made possible by the generous support of the Canada Council for the Arts. Their financial support made possible the exhibition "Living Spaces: The Architecture of Fred Thornton Hollingworth", which took place at the Charles H. Scott Gallery, Emily Carr Institute, Vancouver B.C., from June 9 to July 25, 2004.

**Selwyn Pullan**  A SPECIAL ACKNOWLEDGEMENT MUST GO TO SELWYN PULLAN WHOSE ARCHITECTURAL PHOTOGRAPHS grace many of the pages in this publication. Along with the houses of Fred Hollingsworth, Selwyn Pullan photographed most of the significant architectural work in the west coast region from the 1950's onward. His photographs not only document the architecture; they stand as works of art in their own right. They are a testament to his creative vision and his highly developed technical skill. The strength of his photographs is in their ability to reflect the intent of the architect's design and bring them to life for the viewer. We are grateful for the contribution his images make to this publication.

## Photography Credits

FRED HOLLINGSWORTH
insert: 5, 23, 43, 44, 45, 59, 64, 65, 77, 78, 135, 136, 137, 141, 147, 155, 159, 160

DUFF PAPIN
pages: 15 top, 28, 47

GRAHAM WARRINGTON
pages: 14, 49, 50, 51, 52

BARRY DOWNS
pages: 17, 36, 106, 107, 164, 165, 166, 167, 172, 173, 174, 175

SELWYN PULLAN
pages: 15 bottom, 16, 18, 20, 27, 31, 32, 33, 34, 35, 55, 56, 57, 61, 67, 68, 69, 73, 74, 75, 77, 78, 79, 80, 81, 82, 83, 84, 85, 91, 92, 93, 94, 95, 96, 97, 99, 100, 101, 109, 110, 111, 113, 114, 116, 117, 119, 120, 121, 124, 125, 126, 127, 130, 131, 151, 152, 153

AMELIA BUTLER
pages: 38, 39

The photographs on page 12 are from an unknown source.

All drawings and prespectives by Fred Hollingsworth except Maltby Residence, page 103, by Rob Way.

This publication was supported in part by the Charles H. Scott Gallery, Emily Carr Institute and the Canada Council for the Arts  Canada Council for the Arts    Conseil des Arts du Canada

First published in 2005 by BLUE*IM*PRINT

Essays copyright © 2005 by the Contributors

Book design by Elisa Gutiérrez

Colour separations by Scanlab

Printed and bound in Italy by Grafiche AZ

LIBRARY AND ARCHIVES CANADA CATALOGUING IN PUBLICATION DATA

Hollingsworth, Fred Thornton
   Living Spaces: the architecture of Fred Thornton Hollingsworth.

Includes architectural drawings and plans of Fred Thornton Hollingsworth. Includes an essay by Rhodri Windsor Liscombe and a biography by Greg Bellerby.

ISBN 1-894965-20-5

   1. Hollingsworth, Fred Thornton. I. Liscombe, Rhodri Windsor, 1946- II. Bellerby, Greg L. III. Title.

NA749.H64A4 2005        720'.92      C2004-904609-8